Scope and Closures

Kyle Simpson

Beijing · Cambridge · Farnham · Köln · Sebastopol · Tokyo

Scope and Closures

by Kyle Simpson

Printed in the United States of America.

Published by O'Reilly Media, Inc., 1005 Gravenstein Highway North, Sebastopol, CA 95472.

O'Reilly books may be purchased for educational, business, or sales promotional use. Online editions are also available for most titles (*http://my.safaribooksonline.com*). For more information, contact our corporate/institutional sales department: 800-998-9938 or *corporate@oreilly.com*.

Editors: Simon St. Laurent and Brian Mac-Donald
Production Editor: Melanie Yarbrough
Proofreader: Linley Dolby

Cover Designer: Karen Montgomery
Interior Designer: David Futato
Illustrator: Rebecca Demarest

March 2014:   First Edition

Revision History for the First Edition:

2014-03-06:   First release

See *http://oreilly.com/catalog/errata.csp?isbn=9781449335588* for release details.

ISBN: 978-1-449-33558-8

[LSI]

Table of Contents

Foreword

When I was a young child, I would often enjoy taking things apart and putting them back together again—old mobile phones, hi-fi stereos, and anything else I could get my hands on. I was too young to really use these devices, but whenever one broke, I would instantly ask if I could figure out how it worked.

I remember once looking at a circuit board for an old radio. It had this weird long tube with copper wire wrapped around it. I couldn't work out its purpose, but I immediately went into research mode. What does it do? Why is it in a radio? It doesn't look like the other parts of the circuit board, why? Why does it have copper wrapped around it? What happens if I remove the copper?! Now I know it was a loop antenna, made by wrapping copper wire around a ferrite rod, which are often used in transistor radios.

Did you ever become addicted to figuring out all of the answers to every *why* question? Most children do. In fact it is probably my favorite thing about children—their desire to learn.

Unfortunately, now I'm considered a *professional* and spend my days making things. When I was young, I loved the idea of one day making the things that I took apart. Of course, most things I make now are with JavaScript and not ferrite rods…but close enough! However, despite once loving the idea of making things, I now find myself longing for the desire to figure things out. Sure, I often figure out the best way to solve a problem or fix a bug, but I rarely take the time to question my tools.

And that is exactly why I am so excited about this "You Don't Know JS" series of books. Because it's right. I don't know JS. I use JavaScript day in, day out and have done for many years, but do I really understand it? No. Sure, I understand a lot of it and I often read the specs and the mailing lists, but no, I don't understand as much as my inner six-year-old wishes I did.

Scope and Closures is a brilliant start to the series. It is very well targeted at people like me (and hopefully you, too). It doesn't teach JavaScript as if you've never used it, but it does make you realize how little about the inner workings you probably know. It is also coming out at the perfect time: ES6 is finally settling down and implementation across browsers is going well. If you've not yet made time for learning the new features (such as `let` and `const`), this book will be a great introduction.

So I hope that you enjoy this book, but moreso, that Kyle's way of critically thinking about how every tiny bit of the language works will creep into your mindset and general workflow. Instead of just using the antenna, figure out how and why it works.

—Shane Hudson
www.shanehudson.net

Preface

I'm sure you noticed, but "JS" in the book series title is not an abbreviation for words used to curse about JavaScript, though cursing at the language's quirks is something we can probably all identify with!

From the earliest days of the Web, JavaScript has been a foundational technology that drives interactive experience around the content we consume. While flickering mouse trails and annoying pop-up prompts may be where JavaScript started, nearly two decades later, the technology and capability of JavaScript has grown many orders of magnitude, and few doubt its importance at the heart of the world's most widely available software platform: the Web.

But as a language, it has perpetually been a target for a great deal of criticism, owing partly to its heritage but even more to its design philosophy. Even the name evokes, as Brendan Eich once put it, "dumb kid brother" status next to its more mature older brother, Java. But the name is merely an accident of politics and marketing. The two languages are vastly different in many important ways. "JavaScript" is as related to "Java" as "Carnival" is to "Car."

Because JavaScript borrows concepts and syntax idioms from several languages, including proud C-style procedural roots as well as subtle, less obvious Scheme/Lisp-style functional roots, it is exceedingly approachable to a broad audience of developers, even those with just little to no programming experience. The "Hello World" of JavaScript is so simple that the language is inviting and easy to get comfortable with in early exposure.

While JavaScript is perhaps one of the easiest languages to get up and running with, its eccentricities make solid mastery of the language a vastly less common occurrence than in many other languages. Where it takes a pretty in-depth knowledge of a language like C or C++ to write a full-scale program, full-scale production JavaScript can, and often does, barely scratch the surface of what the language can do.

Sophisticated concepts that are deeply rooted into the language tend instead to surface themselves in *seemingly* simplistic ways, such as passing around functions as callbacks, which encourages the JavaScript developer to just use the language as-is and not worry too much about what's going on under the hood.

It is simultaneously a simple, easy-to-use language that has broad appeal and a complex and nuanced collection of language mechanics that without careful study will elude *true understanding* even for the most seasoned of JavaScript developers.

Therein lies the paradox of JavaScript, the Achilles' heel of the language, the challenge we are presently addressing. Because JavaScript *can* be used without understanding, the understanding of the language is often never attained.

Mission

If at every point that you encounter a surprise or frustration in JavaScript, your response is to add it to the blacklist, as some are accustomed to doing, you soon will be relegated to a hollow shell of the richness of JavaScript.

While this subset has been famoulsy dubbed "The Good Parts," I would implore you, dear reader, to instead consider it the "The Easy Parts," "The Safe Parts," or even "The Incomplete Parts."

This "You Don't Know JavaScript" book series offers a contrary challenge: learn and deeply understand *all* of JavaScript, even and especially "The Tough Parts."

Here, we address head on the tendency of JS developers to learn "just enough" to get by, without ever forcing themselves to learn exactly how and why the language behaves the way it does. Furthermore, we eschew the common advice to *retreat* when the road gets rough.

I am not content, nor should you be, at stopping once something *just works*, and not really knowing *why*. I gently challenge you to journey down that bumpy "road less traveled" and embrace all that JavaScript is and can do. With that knowledge, no technique, no framework, no popular buzzword acronym of the week, will be beyond your understanding.

These books each take on specific core parts of the language that are most commonly misunderstood or under-understood, and dive very deep and exhaustively into them. You should come away from reading with a firm confidence in your understanding, not just of the theoretical, but the practical "what you need to know" bits.

The JavaScript you know *right now* is probably *parts* handed down to you by others who've been burned by incomplete understanding. *That* JavaScript is but a shadow of the true language. You don't *really* know JavaScript, *yet*, but if you dig into this series, you *will*. Read on, my friends. JavaScript awaits you.

Review

JavaScript is awesome. It's easy to learn partially, but much harder to learn completely (or even *sufficiently*). When developers encounter confusion, they usually blame the language instead of their lack of understanding. These books aim to fix that, inspiring a strong appreciation for the language you can now, and *should*, deeply *know*.

 Many of the examples in this book assume modern (and future-reaching) JavaScript engine environments, such as ECMA-Script version 6 (ES6). Some code may not work as described if run in older (pre-ES6) environments.

Conventions Used in This Book

The following typographical conventions are used in this book:

Italic
> Indicates new terms, URLs, email addresses, filenames, and file extensions.

`Constant width`
> Used for program listings, as well as within paragraphs to refer to program elements such as variable or function names, databases, data types, environment variables, statements, and keywords.

Constant width bold

> Shows commands or other text that should be typed literally by the user.

Constant width italic

> Shows text that should be replaced with user-supplied values or by values determined by context.

 This element signifies a tip or suggestion.

 This element signifies a general note.

 This element indicates a warning or caution.

Using Code Examples

Supplemental material (code examples, exercises, etc.) is available for download at *http://bit.ly/1c8HEWF*.

This book is here to help you get your job done. In general, if example code is offered with this book, you may use it in your programs and documentation. You do not need to contact us for permission unless you're reproducing a significant portion of the code. For example, writing a program that uses several chunks of code from this book does not require permission. Selling or distributing a CD-ROM of examples from O'Reilly books does require permission. Answering a question by citing this book and quoting example code does not require permission. Incorporating a significant amount of example code from this book into your product's documentation does require permission.

We appreciate, but do not require, attribution. An attribution usually includes the title, author, publisher, and ISBN. For example: "*Scope and Closures* by Kyle Simpson (O'Reilly). Copyright 2014 Kyle Simpson, 978-1-449-33558-8."

If you feel your use of code examples falls outside fair use or the permission given above, feel free to contact us at *permissions@oreilly.com*.

Safari® Books Online

Safari Books Online is an on-demand digital library that delivers expert content in both book and video form from the world's leading authors in technology and business.

Technology professionals, software developers, web designers, and business and creative professionals use Safari Books Online as their primary resource for research, problem solving, learning, and certification training.

Safari Books Online offers a range of product mixes and pricing programs for organizations, government agencies, and individuals. Subscribers have access to thousands of books, training videos, and prepublication manuscripts in one fully searchable database from publishers like O'Reilly Media, Prentice Hall Professional, Addison-Wesley Professional, Microsoft Press, Sams, Que, Peachpit Press, Focal Press, Cisco Press, John Wiley & Sons, Syngress, Morgan Kaufmann, IBM Redbooks, Packt, Adobe Press, FT Press, Apress, Manning, New Riders, McGraw-Hill, Jones & Bartlett, Course Technology, and dozens more. For more information about Safari Books Online, please visit us online.

How to Contact Us

Please address comments and questions concerning this book to the publisher:

O'Reilly Media, Inc.
1005 Gravenstein Highway North
Sebastopol, CA 95472
800-998-9938 (in the United States or Canada)
707-829-0515 (international or local)
707-829-0104 (fax)

We have a web page for this book, where we list errata, examples, and any additional information. You can access this page at *http://oreil.ly/ JS_scope_and_closures*.

To comment or ask technical questions about this book, send email to *bookquestions@oreilly.com*.

For more information about our books, courses, conferences, and news, see our website at *http://www.oreilly.com*.

Find us on Facebook: *http://facebook.com/oreilly*

Follow us on Twitter: *http://twitter.com/oreillymedia*

Watch us on YouTube: *http://www.youtube.com/oreillymedia*

Check out the full *You Don't Know JS* series: *http://YouDont KnowJS.com*

CHAPTER 1

What Is Scope?

One of the most fundamental paradigms of nearly all programming languages is the ability to store values in variables, and later retrieve or modify those values. In fact, the ability to store values and pull values out of variables is what gives a program *state*.

Without such a concept, a program could perform some tasks, but they would be extremely limited and not terribly interesting.

But the inclusion of variables into our program begets the most interesting questions we will now address: where do those variables *live*? In other words, where are they stored? And, most important, how does our program find them when it needs them?

These questions speak to the need for a well-defined set of rules for storing variables in some location, and for finding those variables at a later time. We'll call that set of rules: *scope*.

What Is Scope?

But, where and how do these *scope* rules get set?

Compiler Theory

It may be self-evident, or it may be surprising, depending on your level of interaction with various languages, but despite the fact that JavaScript falls under the general category of "dynamic" or "interpreted" languages, it is in fact a compiled language. It is *not* compiled well in advance, as are many traditionally compiled languages, nor are the results of compilation portable among various distributed systems.

But, nevertheless, the JavaScript engine performs many of the same steps, albeit in more sophisticated ways than we may commonly be aware, of any traditional language compiler.

In traditional compiled-language process, a chunk of source code, your program, will undergo typically three steps *before* it is executed, roughly called "compilation":

Tokenizing/Lexing
Breaking up a string of characters into meaningful (to the language) chunks, called tokens. For instance, consider the program var a = 2;. This program would likely be broken up into the following tokens: var, a, =, 2, and ;. Whitespace may or may not be persisted as a token, depending on whether its meaningful or not.

The difference between tokenizing and lexing is subtle and academic, but it centers on whether or not these tokens are identified in a *stateless* or *stateful* way. Put simply, if the tokenizer were to invoke stateful parsing rules to figure out whether a should be considered a distinct token or just part of another token, *that* would be *lexing*.

Parsing
taking a stream (array) of tokens and turning it into a tree of nested elements, which collectively represent the grammatical structure of the program. This tree is called an "AST" (*abstract syntax tree*).

The tree for var a = 2; might start with a top-level node called VariableDeclaration, with a child node called Identifier (whose value is a), and another child called AssignmentExpres sion, which itself has a child called NumericLiteral (whose value is 2).

Code-Generation
The process of taking an AST and turning it into executable code. This part varies greatly depending on the language, the platform it's targeting, and so on.

So, rather than get mired in details, we'll just handwave and say that there's a way to take our previously described AST for var a = 2; and turn it into a set of machine instructions to actually *create* a variable called a (including reserving memory, etc.), and then store a value into a.

 The details of how the engine manages system resources are deeper than we will dig, so we'll just take it for granted that the engine is able to create and store variables as needed.

The JavaScript engine is vastly more complex than *just* those three steps, as are most other language compilers. For instance, in the process of parsing and code-generation, there are certainly steps to optimize the performance of the execution, including collapsing redundant elements, etc.

So, I'm painting only with broad strokes here. But I think you'll see shortly why these details we *do* cover, even at a high level, are relevant.

For one thing, JavaScript engines don't get the luxury (like other language compilers) of having plenty of time to optimize, because Java-Script compilation doesn't happen in a build step ahead of time, as with other languages.

For JavaScript, the compilation that occurs happens, in many cases, mere microseconds (or less!) before the code is executed. To ensure the fastest performance, JS engines use all kinds of tricks (like JITs, which lazy compile and even hot recompile, etc.) that are well beyond the "scope" of our discussion here.

Let's just say, for simplicity sake, that any snippet of JavaScript has to be compiled before (usually *right* before!) it's executed. So, the JS compiler will take the program var a = 2; and compile it *first*, and then be ready to execute it, usually right away.

Understanding Scope

The way we will approach learning about scope is to think of the process in terms of a conversation. But, *who* is having the conversation?

The Cast

Let's meet the cast of characters that interact to process the program var a = 2;, so we understand their conversations that we'll listen in on shortly:

Engine
>Responsible for start-to-finish compilation and execution of our JavaScript program.

Compiler
>One of Engine's friends; handles all the dirty work of parsing and code-generation (see previous section).

Scope
>Another friend of Engine; collects and maintains a look-up list of all the declared identifiers (variables), and enforces a strict set of rules as to how these are accessible to currently executing code.

For you to *fully understand* how JavaScript works, you need to begin to *think* like Engine (and friends) think, ask the questions they ask, and answer those questions the same.

Back and Forth

When you see the program var a = 2;, you most likely think of that as one statement. But that's not how our new friend Engine sees it. In fact, Engine sees two distinct statements, one that Compiler will handle during compilation, and one that Engine will handle during execution.

So, let's break down how Engine and friends will approach the program var a = 2;.

The first thing Compiler will do with this program is perform lexing to break it down into tokens, which it will then parse into a tree. But when Compiler gets to code generation, it will treat this program somewhat differently than perhaps assumed.

A reasonable assumption would be that Compiler will produce code that could be summed up by this pseudocode: "Allocate memory for a variable, label it a, then stick the value 2 into that variable." Unfortunately, that's not quite accurate.

Compiler will instead proceed as:

1. Encountering var a, Compiler asks Scope to see if a variable a already exists for that particular scope collection. If so, Compiler ignores this declaration and moves on. Otherwise, Compiler asks Scope to declare a new variable called a for that scope collection.

2. Compiler then produces code for Engine to later execute, to handle the a = 2 assignment. The code Engine runs will first ask Scope

if there is a variable called a accessible in the current scope collection. If so, Engine uses that variable. If not, Engine looks *elsewhere* (see "Nested Scope" on page 8).

If Engine eventually finds a variable, it assigns the value 2 to it. If not, Engine will raise its hand and yell out an error!

To summarize: two distinct actions are taken for a variable assignment: First, Compiler declares a variable (if not previously declared) in the current Scope, and second, when executing, Engine looks up the variable in Scope and assigns to it, if found.

[handwritten margin note: How does the Engine & Compiler Execute code?]

Compiler Speak

We need a little bit more compiler terminology to proceed further with understanding.

When Engine executes the code that Compiler produced for step 2, it has to look up the variable a to see if it has been declared, and this look-up is consulting Scope. But the type of look-up Engine performs affects the outcome of the look-up.

In our case, it is said that Engine would be performing an LHS look-up for the variable a. The other type of look-up is called RHS.

I bet you can guess what the "L" and "R" mean. These terms stand for lefthand side and righthand side.

Side...of what? *Of an assignment operation.*

In other words, an LHS look-up is done when a variable appears on the lefthand side of an assignment operation, and an RHS look-up is done when a variable appears on the righthand side of an assignment operation.

Actually, let's be a little more precise. An RHS look-up is indistinguishable, for our purposes, from simply a look-up of the value of some variable, whereas the LHS look-up is trying to find the variable container itself, so that it can assign. In this way, RHS doesn't *really* mean "righthand side of an assignment" per se, it just, more accurately, means "not lefthand side".

Being slightly glib for a moment, you could think RHS instead means "retrieve his/her source (value)," implying that RHS means "go get the value of..."

Let's dig into that deeper.

When I say:

[handwritten: nothing being assigned → we're looking to retrieve the value of A]

```
console.log( a );
```

[handwritten left margin: RHS —]

The reference to a is an RHS reference, because nothing is being assigned to a here. Instead, we're looking up to retrieve the value of a, so that the value can be passed to console.log(..).

By contrast:

[handwritten left margin: LHS —]

```
a = 2;
```

The reference to a here is an LHS reference, because we don't actually care what the current value is, we simply want to find the variable as a target for the = 2 assignment operation.

LHS and RHS meaning "left/righthand side of an assigment" doesn't necessarily literally mean "left/right side of the = assignment operator." There are several other ways that assignments happen, and so it's better to conceptually think about it as: "Who's the target of the assignment (LHS)?" and "Who's the source of the assignment (RHS)?"

Consider this program, which has both LHS and RHS references:

[handwritten: a = 2 — LHS]

```
function foo(a) {
    console.log( a ); // 2
}
foo( 2 );
```

[handwritten: RHS (on console.log line)]

[handwritten: RHS — foo(2); → Go look up the value of foo & give it to me]

The last line that invokes foo(..) as a function call requires an RHS reference to foo, meaning, "Go look up the value of foo, and give it to me." Moreover, (..) means the value of foo should be executed, so it'd better actually be a function!

There's a subtle but important assignment here.

You may have missed the implied a = 2 in this code snippet. It happens when the value 2 is passed as an argument to the foo(..) function, in which case the 2 value is *assigned* to the parameter a. To (implicitly) assign to parameter a, an LHS look-up is performed.

There's also an RHS reference for the value of a, and that resulting value is passed to console.log(..). console.log(..) needs a reference to execute. It's an RHS look-up for the console object, then a property resolution occurs to see if it has a method called log.

Finally, we can conceptualize that there's an LHS/RHS exchange of passing the value 2 (by way of variable a's RHS look-up) into log(..). Inside of the native implementation of log(..), we can assume it has parameters, the first of which (perhaps called arg1) has an LHS reference look-up, before assigning 2 to it.

 You might be tempted to conceptualize the function declaration function foo(a) {... as a normal variable declaration and assignment, such as var foo and foo = function(a){.... In so doing, it would be tempting to think of this function declaration as involving an LHS look-up.

However, the subtle but important difference is that Compiler handles both the declaration and the value definition during code-generation, such that when Engine is executing code, there's no processing necessary to "assign" a function value to foo. Thus, it's not really appropriate to think of a function declaration as an LHS look-up assignment in the way we're discussing them here.

Engine/Scope Conversation

```
function foo(a) {
    console.log( a ); // 2
}

foo( 2 );
```

Let's imagine the above exchange (which processes this code snippet) as a conversation. The conversation would go a little something like this:

Engine: Hey Scope, I have an RHS reference for foo. Ever heard of it?

Scope: Why yes, I have. Compiler declared it just a second ago. It's a function. Here you go.

Engine: Great, thanks! OK, I'm executing foo.

Engine: Hey, Scope, I've got an LHS reference for a, ever heard of it?

Scope: Why yes, I have. Compiler declared it as a formal parameter to foo just recently. Here you go.

Engine: Helpful as always, Scope. Thanks again. Now, time to assign 2 to a.

Engine: Hey, Scope, sorry to bother you again. I need an RHS look-up for console. Ever heard of it?

Scope: No problem, Engine, this is what I do all day. Yes, I've got console. It's built-in. Here ya go.

Engine: Perfect. Looking up log(..). OK, great, it's a function.

Engine: Yo, Scope. Can you help me out with an RHS reference to a. I think I remember it, but just want to double-check.

Scope: You're right, Engine. Same variable, hasn't changed. Here ya go.

Engine: Cool. Passing the value of a, which is 2, into log(..).

...

Quiz

Check your understanding so far. Make sure to play the part of Engine and have a "conversation" with Scope:

```
function foo(a) {
    var b = a;
    return a + b;
}

var c = foo( 2 );
```

1. Identify all the LHS look-ups (there are 3!).

2. Identify all the RHS look-ups (there are 4!).

 See the chapter review for the quiz answers!

Nested Scope

We said that Scope is a set of rules for looking up variables by their identifier name. There's usually more than one scope to consider, however.

Just as a block or function is nested inside another block or function, scopes are nested inside other scopes. So, if a variable cannot be found in the immediate scope, Engine consults the next outercontaining scope, continuing until is found or until the outermost (a.k.a., global) scope has been reached.

Consider the following:

```
function foo(a) {
    console.log( a + b );
}

var b = 2;

foo( 2 ); // 4
```

The RHS reference for b cannot be resolved inside the function foo, but it can be resolved in the scope surrounding it (in this case, the global).

So, revisiting the conversations between Engine and Scope, we'd overhear:

> Engine: "Hey, Scope of foo, ever heard of b? Got an RHS reference for it."
>
> Scope: "Nope, never heard of it. Go fish."
>
> Engine: "Hey, Scope outside of foo, oh you're the global scope, OK cool. Ever heard of b? Got an RHS reference for it."
>
> Scope: "Yep, sure have. Here ya go."

The simple rules for traversing nested scope: Engine starts at the currently executing scope, looks for the variable there, then if not found, keeps going up one level, and so on. If the outermost global scope is reached, the search stops, whether it finds the variable or not.

Building on Metaphors

To visualize the process of nested scope resolution, I want you to think of this tall building:

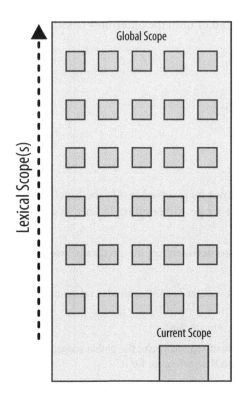

The building represents our program's nested scope ruleset. The first floor of the building represents your currently executing scope, wherever you are. The top level of the building is the global scope.

You resolve LHS and RHS references by looking on your current floor, and if you don't find it, taking the elevator to the next floor, looking there, then the next, and so on. Once you get to the top floor (the global scope), you either find what you're looking for, or you don't. But you have to stop regardless.

Errors

Why does it matter whether we call it LHS or RHS?

Because these two types of look-ups behave differently in the circumstance where the variable has not yet been declared (is not found in any consulted scope).

Consider:

```
function foo(a) {
    console.log( a + b );
    b = a;
}

foo( 2 );
```

When the RHS look-up occurs for b the first time, it will not be found. This is said to be an "undeclared" variable, because it is not found in the scope.

If an RHS look-up fails to ever find a variable, anywhere in the nested scopes, this results in a `ReferenceError` being thrown by the engine. It's important to note that the error is of the type `ReferenceError`.

By contrast, if the engine is performing an LHS look-up, and it arrives at the top floor (global scope) without finding it, if the program is not running in "Strict Mode,"[1] then the global scope will create a new variable of that name *in the global scope*, and hand it back to Engine.

"No, there wasn't one before, but I was helpful and created one for you."

"Strict Mode," which was added in ES5, has a number of different behaviors from normal/relaxed/lazy mode. One such behavior is that it disallows the automatic/implicit global variable creation. In that case, there would be no global scoped variable to hand back from an LHS look-up, and Engine would throw a `ReferenceError` similarly to the RHS case.

Now, if a variable is found for an RHS look-up, but you try to do something with its value that is impossible, such as trying to execute-as-function a nonfunction value, or reference a property on a `null` or `undefined` value, then Engine throws a different kind of error, called a `TypeError`.

`ReferenceError` is scope resolution-failure related, whereas `TypeError` implies that scope resolution was successful, but that there was an illegal/impossible action attempted against the result.

Review

Scope is the set of rules that determines where and how a variable (identifier) can be looked up. This look-up may be for the purposes of

---

1. See the MDN's break down of Strict Mode (*http://mzl.la/1epvZNQ*)

assigning to the variable, which is an LHS (lefthand-side) reference, or it may be for the purposes of retrieving its value, which is an RHS (righthand-side) reference.

LHS references result from assignment operations. Scope-related assignments can occur either with the = operator or by passing arguments to (assign to) function parameters.

The JavaScript engine first compiles code before it executes, and in so doing, it splits up statements like var a = 2; into two separate steps:

1. First, var a to declare it in that scope. This is performed at the beginning, before code execution.

2. Later, a = 2 to look up the variable (LHS reference) and assign to it if found.

Both LHS and RHS reference look-ups start at the currently executing scope, and if need be (that is, they don't find what they're looking for there), they work their way up the nested scope, one scope (floor) at a time, looking for the identifier, until they get to the global (top floor) and stop, and either find it, or don't.

Unfulfilled RHS references result in `ReferenceErrors` being thrown. Unfulfilled LHS references result in an automatic, implicitly created global of that name (if not in Strict Mode), or a `ReferenceError` (if in Strict Mode).

Quiz Answers

```
function foo(a) {
    var b = a;
    return a + b;
}

var c = foo( 2 );
```

1. Identify all the LHS look-ups (there are 3!).

   `c = ..;, a = 2 (implicit param assignment) and b = ..`

2. Identify all the RHS look-ups (there are 4!).

   `foo(2.., = a;, a .. and .. b`

CHAPTER 2

Lexical Scope

In Chapter 1, we defined "scope" as the set of rules that govern how the engine can look up a variable by its identifier name and find it, either in the current scope, or in any of the nested scopes it's contained within.

There are two predominant models for how scope works. The first of these is by far the most common, used by the vast majority of programming languages. It's called *lexical scope*, and we will examine it in depth. The other model, which is still used by some languages (such as Bash scripting, some modes in Perl, etc) is called *dynamic scope*.

Dynamic scope is covered in Appendix A. I mention it here only to provide a contrast with lexical scope, which is the scope model that JavaScript employs.

Lex-time

As we discussed in Chapter 1, the first traditional phase of a standard language compiler is called lexing (a.k.a., tokenizing). If you recall, the lexing process examines a string of source code characters and assigns semantic meaning to the tokens as a result of some stateful parsing.

It is this concept that provides the foundation to understand what lexical scope is and where the name comes from.

To define it somewhat circularly, lexical scope is scope that is defined at lexing time. In other words, lexical scope is based on where variables and blocks of scope are authored, by you, at write time, and thus is (mostly) set in stone by the time the lexer processes your code.

We will see in a little bit that there are some ways to cheat lexical scope, thereby modifying it after the lexer has passed by, but these are frowned upon. It is considered best practice to treat lexical scope as, in fact, lexical-only, and thus entirely author-time in nature.

Let's consider this block of code:

```
function foo(a) {

    var b = a * 2;

    function bar(c) {
        console.log( a, b, c );
    }

    bar( b * 3 );
}

foo( 2 ); // 2, 4, 12
```

There are three nested scopes inherent in this code example. It may be helpful to think about these scopes as bubbles inside of each other.

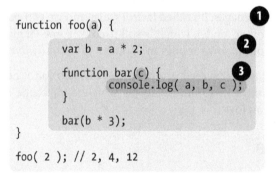

Bubble 1 encompasses the global scope and has just one identifier in it: foo.

Bubble 2 encompasses the scope of foo, which includes the three identifiers: a, bar, and b.

Bubble 3 encompasses the scope of bar, and it includes just one identifier: c.

Scope bubbles are defined by where the blocks of scope are written, which one is nested inside the other, etc. In the next chapter, we'll discuss different units of scope, but for now, let's just assume that each function creates a new bubble of scope.

The bubble for bar is entirely contained within the bubble for foo, because (and only because) that's where we chose to define the function bar.

Notice that these nested bubbles are strictly nested. We're not talking about Venn diagrams where the bubbles can cross boundaries. In other words, no bubble for some function can simultaneously exist (partially) inside two other outer scope bubbles, just as no function can partially be inside each of two parent functions.

Look-ups

The structure and relative placement of these scope bubbles fully explains to the engine all the places it needs to look to find an identifier.

In the previous code snippet, the engine executes the con sole.log(..) statement and goes looking for the three referenced variables a, b, and c. It first starts with the innermost scope bubble, the scope of the bar(..) function. It won't find a there, so it goes up one level, out to the next nearest scope bubble, the scope of foo(..). It finds a there, and so it uses that a. Same thing for b. But c, it does find inside of bar(..).

Had there been a c both inside of bar(..) and inside of foo(..), the console.log(..) statement would have found and used the one in bar(..), never getting to the one in foo(..).

Scope look-up stops once it finds the first match. The same identifier name can be specified at multiple layers of nested scope, which is called "shadowing" (the inner identifer "shadows" the outer identifier). Regardless of shadowing, scope look-up always starts at the innermost scope being executed at the time, and works its way outward/upward until the first match, and stops.

Global variables are automatically also properties of the global object (`window` in browsers, etc.), so it *is* possible to reference a global variable not directly by its lexical name, but instead indirectly as a property reference of the global object.

`window.a`

This technique gives access to a global variable that would otherwise be inaccessible due to it being shadowed. However, non-global shadowed variables cannot be accessed.

No matter *where* a function is invoked from, or even *how* it is invoked, its lexical scope is *only* defined by where the function was declared.

The lexical scope look-up process *only* applies to first-class identifiers, such as the a, b, and c. If you had a reference to `foo.bar.baz` in a piece of code, the lexical scope look-up would apply to finding the `foo` identifier, but once it locates that variable, object property-access rules take over to resolve the `bar` and `baz` properties, respectively.

Cheating Lexical

If lexical scope is defined only by where a function is declared, which is entirely an author-time decision, how could there possibly be a way to "modify" (a.k.a., cheat) lexical scope at runtime?

JavaScript has two such mechanisms. Both of them are equally frowned upon in the wider community as bad practices to use in your code. But the typical arguments against them are often missing the most important point: *cheating lexical scope leads to poorer performance*.

Before I explain the performance issue, though, let's look at how these two mechanisms work.

eval

The `eval(..)` function in JavaScript takes a string as an argument and treats the contents of the string as if it had actually been authored code at that point in the program. In other words, you can programatically generate code inside of your authored code, and run the generated code as if it had been there at author time.

Evaluating `eval(..)` (pun intended) in that light, it should be clear how `eval(..)` allows you to modify the lexical scope environment by cheating and pretending that author-time (a.k.a., lexical) code was there all along.

On subsequent lines of code after an eval(..) has executed, the engine will not "know" or "care" that the previous code in question was dynamically interpreted and thus modified the lexical scope environment. The engine will simply perform its lexical scope lookups as it always does.

Consider the following code:

```
function foo(str, a) {
    eval( str ); // cheating!
    console.log( a, b );
}

var b = 2;

foo( "var b = 3;", 1 ); // 1, 3
```

The string "var b = 3;" is treated, at the point of the eval(..) call, as code that was there all along. Because that code happens to declare a new variable b, it modifies the existing lexical scope of foo(..). In fact, as mentioned earlier, this code actually creates variable b inside of foo(..) that shadows the b that was declared in the outer (global) scope.

When the console.log(..) call occurs, it finds both a and b in the scope of foo(..), and never finds the outer b. Thus, we print out "1, 3" instead of "1, 2" as would have normally been the case.

 In this example, for simplicity sake, the string of "code" we pass in was a fixed literal. But it could easily have been programatically created by adding characters together based on your program's logic. eval(..) is usually used to execute dynamically created code, as dynamically evaluating essentially static code from a string literal would provide no real benefit to just authoring the code directly.

By default, if a string of code that eval(..) executes contains one or more declarations (either variables or functions), this action modifies the existing lexical scope in which the eval(..) resides. Technically, eval(..) can be invoked indirectly, through various tricks (beyond our discussion here), which causes it to instead execute in the context of the global scope, thus modifying it. But in either case, eval(..) can at runtime modify an author-time lexical scope.

eval(..) when used in a strict-mode program operates in its own lexical scope, which means declarations made inside of the eval() do not actually modify the enclosing scope.

```
function foo(str) {
    "use strict";
    eval( str );
    console.log( a ); // ReferenceError: a is not defined
}

foo( "var a = 2" );
```

There are other facilities in JavaScript that amount to a very similar effect to eval(..). setTimeout(..) and setInterval(..) *can* take a string for their respective first argument, the contents of which are evaluated as the code of a dynamically generated function. This is old, legacy behavior and long-since deprecated. Don't do it!

The new Function(..) function constructor similarly takes a string of code in its *last* argument to turn into a dynamically generated function (the first argument(s), if any, are the named parameters for the new function). This function-constructor syntax is slightly safer than eval(..), but it should still be avoided in your code.

The use-cases for dynamically generating code inside your program are incredibly rare, as the performance degradations are almost never worth the capability.

with

The other frowned-upon (and now deprecated!) feature in JavaScript that cheats lexical scope is the with keyword. There are multiple valid ways that with can be explained, but I will choose here to explain it from the perspective of how it interacts with and affects lexical scope.

with is typically explained as a shorthand for making multiple property references against an object *without* repeating the object reference itself each time.

For example:

```
var obj = {
    a: 1,
    b: 2,
```

```
        c: 3
};

// more "tedious" to repeat "obj"
obj.a = 2;
obj.b = 3;
obj.c = 4;

// "easier" short-hand
with (obj) {
    a = 3;
    b = 4;
    c = 5;
}
```

However, there's much more going on here than just a convenient
shorthand for object property access. Consider:

```
function foo(obj) {
    with (obj) {
        a = 2;
    }
}

var o1 = {
    a: 3
};

var o2 = {
    b: 3
};

foo( o1 );
console.log( o1.a ); // 2

foo( o2 );
console.log( o2.a ); // undefined
console.log( a ); // 2—Oops, leaked global!
```

In this code example, two objects o1 and o2 are created. One has an a
property, and the other does not. The foo(..) function takes an object
reference obj as an argument, and calls with (obj) { .. } on the
reference. Inside the with block, we make what appears to be a normal
lexical reference to a variable a, an LHS reference in fact (see Chapter 1), to assign to it the value of 2.

When we pass in o1, the a = 2 assignment finds the property o1.a
and assigns it the value 2, as reflected in the subsequent con
sole.log(o1.a) statement. However, when we pass in o2, since it does

not have an a property, no such property is created, and o2.a remains undefined.

But then we note a peculiar side-effect, the fact that a global variable a was created by the a = 2 assignment. How can this be?

The with statement takes an object, one that has zero or more properties, and treats that object as if it is a wholly separate lexical scope, and thus the object's properties are treated as lexically defined identifiers in that scope.

 Even though a with block treats an object like a lexical scope, a normal var declaration inside that with block will not be scoped to that with block, but instead the containing function scope.

While the eval(..) function can modify existing lexical scope if it takes a string of code with one or more declarations in it, the with statement actually creates a *whole new lexical scope* out of thin air, from the object you pass to it.

Understood in this way, the scope declared by the with statement when we passed in o1 was o1, and that scope had an identifier in it which corresponds to the o1.a property. But when we used o2 as the scope, it had no such a identifier in it, and so the normal rules of LHS identifier look-up (see Chapter 1) occurred.

Neither the scope of o2, nor the scope of foo(..), nor the global scope even, has an a identifier to be found, so when a = 2 is executed, it results in the automatic global being created (since we're in non-strict mode).

It is a strange sort of mind-bending thought to see with turning, at runtime, an object and its properties into a scope *with* identifiers. But that is the clearest explanation I can give for the results we see.

 In addition to being a bad idea to use, both eval(..) and with are affected (restricted) by Strict Mode. with is outright disallowed, whereas various forms of indirect or unsafe eval(..) are disallowed while retaining the core functionality.

Performance

Both `eval(..)` and `with` cheat the otherwise author-time defined lexical scope by modifying or creating new lexical scope at runtime.

So, what's the big deal, you ask? If they offer more sophisticated functionality and coding flexibility, aren't these *good* features? *No.*

The JavaScript engine has a number of performance optimizations that it performs during the compilation phase. Some of these boil down to being able to essentially statically analyze the code as it lexes, and predetermine where all the variable and function declarations are, so that it takes less effort to resolve identifiers during execution.

But if the engine finds an `eval(..)` or `with` in the code, it essentially has to *assume* that all its awareness of identifier location may be invalid, because it cannot know at lexing time exactly what code you may pass to `eval(..)` to modify the lexical scope, or the contents of the object you may pass to `with` to create a new lexical scope to be consulted.

In other words, in the pessimistic sense, most of those optimizations it *would* make are pointless if `eval(..)` or `with` are present, so it simply doesn't perform the optimizations *at all*.

Your code will almost certainly tend to run slower simply by the fact that you include an `eval(..)` or `with` anywhere in the code. No matter how smart the engine may be about trying to limit the side-effects of these pessmistic assumptions, **there's no getting around the fact that without the optimizations, code runs slower.**

Review

Lexical scope means that scope is defined by author-time decisions of where functions are declared. The lexing phase of compilation is essentially able to know where and how all identifiers are declared, and thus predict how they will be looked up during execution.

Two mechanisms in JavaScript can "cheat" lexical scope: `eval(..)` and `with`. The former can modify existing lexical scope (at runtime) by evaluating a string of "code" that has one or more declarations in it. The latter essentially creates a whole new lexical scope (again, at runtime) by treating an object reference *as* a scope and that object's properties as scoped identifiers.

The downside to these mechanisms is that it defeats the engine's ability to perform compile-time optimizations regarding scope look-up, because the engine has to assume pessimistically that such optimizations will be invalid. Code *will* run slower as a result of using either feature. *Don't use them.*

CHAPTER 3

Function Versus Block Scope

As we explored in Chapter 2, scope consists of a series of "bubbles" that each act as a container or bucket, in which identifiers (variables, functions) are declared. These bubbles nest neatly inside each other, and this nesting is defined at author time.

But what exactly makes a new bubble? Is it only the function? Can other structures in JavaScript create bubbles of scope?

Scope From Functions

The most common answer to those questions is that JavaScript has function-based scope. That is, each function you declare creates a bubble for itself, but no other structures create their own scope bubbles. As we'll see in just a little bit, this is not quite true.

But first, let's explore function scope and its implications.

Consider this code:

```
function foo(a) {
    var b = 2;

    // some code

    function bar() {
        // ...
    }

    // more code

    var c = 3;
}
```

In this snippet, the scope bubble for foo(..) includes identifiers a, b, c, and bar. It doesn't matter *where* in the scope a declaration appears, the variable or function belongs to the containing scope bubble, regardless. We'll explore how exactly *that* works in the next chapter.

bar(..) has its own scope bubble. So does the global scope, which has just one identifier attached to it: foo.

Because a, b, c, and bar all belong to the scope bubble of foo(..), they are not accessible outside of foo(..). That is, the following code would all result in ReferenceError errors, as the identifiers are not available to the global scope:

```
bar(); // fails

console.log( a, b, c ); // all 3 fail
```

However, all these identifiers (a, b, c, foo, and bar) are accessible *inside* of foo(..), and indeed also available inside of bar(..) (assuming there are no shadow identifier declarations inside bar(..)).

Function scope encourages the idea that all variables belong to the function, and can be used and reused throughout the entirety of the function (and indeed, accessible even to nested scopes). This design approach can be quite useful, and certainly can make full use of the "dynamic" nature of JavaScript variables to take on values of different types as needed.

On the other hand, if you don't take careful precautions, variables existing across the entirety of a scope can lead to some unexpected pitfalls.

Hiding in Plain Scope

The traditional way of thinking about functions is that you declare a function and then add code inside it. But the inverse thinking is equally powerful and useful: take any arbitrary section of code you've written and wrap a function declaration around it, which in effect "hides" the code.

The practical result is to create a scope bubble around the code in question, which means that any declarations (variable or function) in that code will now be tied to the scope of the new wrapping function, rather than the previously enclosing scope. In other words, you can "hide" variables and functions by enclosing them in the scope of a function.

Why would "hiding" variables and functions be a useful technique?

There's a variety of reasons motivating this scope-based hiding. They tend to arise from the software design principle Principle of Least Privilege[1], also sometimes called Least Authority or Least Exposure. This principle states that in the design of software, such as the API for a module/object, you should expose only what is minimally necessary, and "hide" everything else.

This principle extends to the choice of which scope to contain variables and functions. If all variables and functions were in the global scope, they would of course be accessible to any nested scope. But this would violate the "Least..." principle in that you are (likely) exposing many variables or functions that you should otherwise keep private, as proper use of the code would discourage access to those variables/functions.

For example:

```
function doSomething(a) {
    b = a + doSomethingElse( a * 2 );

    console.log( b * 3 );
}

function doSomethingElse(a) {
    return a - 1;
}

var b;

doSomething( 2 ); // 15
```

In this snippet, the b variable and the doSomethingElse(..) function are likely "private" details of how doSomething(..) does its job. Giving the enclosing scope "access" to b and doSomethingElse(..) is not only unnecessary but also possibly "dangerous," in that they may be used in unexpected ways, intentionally or not, and this may violate precondition assumptions of doSomething(..). A more "proper" design would hide these private details inside the scope of doSometh ing(..), such as:

---

1. Principle of Least Privilege (*http://bit.ly/1hhrWYC*)

```
function doSomething(a) {
    function doSomethingElse(a) {
        return a - 1;
    }

    var b;

    b = a + doSomethingElse( a * 2 );

    console.log( b * 3 );
}

doSomething( 2 ); // 15
```

Now, b and doSomethingElse(..) are not accessible to any outside influence, instead controlled only by doSomething(..). The functionality and end result has not been affected, but the design keeps private details private, which is usually considered better software.

Collision Avoidance

Another benefit of "hiding" variables and functions inside a scope is to avoid unintended collision between two different identifiers with the same name but different intended usages. Collision results often in unexpected overwriting of values.

For example:

```
function foo() {
    function bar(a) {
        i = 3; // changing the `i` in the enclosing scope's
               // for-loop
        console.log( a + i );
    }

    for (var i=0; i<10; i++) {
        bar( i * 2 ); // oops, inifinite loop ahead!
    }
}

foo();
```

The i = 3 assignment inside of bar(..) overwrites, unexpectedly, the i that was declared in foo(..) at the for loop. In this case, it will result in an infinite loop, because i is set to a fixed value of 3 and that will forever remain < 10.

The assignment inside bar(..) needs to declare a local variable to use, regardless of what identifier name is chosen. var i = 3; would fix the problem (and would create the previously mentioned "shadowed variable" declaration for i). An *additional*, not alternate, option is to pick another identifier name entirely, such as var j = 3;. But your software design may naturally call for the same identifier name, so utilizing scope to "hide" your inner declaration is your best/only option in that case.

Global namespaces

A particularly strong example of (likely) variable collision occurs in the global scope. Multiple libraries loaded into your program can quite easily collide with each other if they don't properly hide their internal/ private functions and variables.

Such libraries typically will create a single variable declaration, often an object, with a sufficiently unique name, in the global scope. This object is then used as a *namespace* for that library, where all specific exposures of functionality are made as properties off that object (namespace), rather than as top-level lexically scoped identifiers themselves.

For example:

```
var MyReallyCoolLibrary = {
    awesome: "stuff",
    doSomething: function() {
        // ...
    },
    doAnotherThing: function() {
        // ...
    }
};
```

Module management

Another option for collision avoidance is the more modern *module* approach, using any of various dependency managers. Using these tools, no libraries ever add any identifiers to the global scope, but are instead required to have their identifier(s) be explicitly imported into another specific scope through usage of the dependency manager's various mechanisms.

It should be observed that these tools do not possess "magic" functionality that is exempt from lexical scoping rules. They simply use the rules of scoping as explained here to enforce that no identifiers are injected into any shared scope, and are instead kept in private, non-collision-susceptible scopes, which prevents any accidental scope collisions.

As such, you can code defensively and achieve the same results as the dependency managers do without actually needing to use them, if you so choose. See the Chapter 5 for more information about the module pattern.

Functions as Scopes

We've seen that we can take any snippet of code and wrap a function around it, and that effectively "hides" any enclosed variable or function declarations from the outside scope inside that function's inner scope.

For example:

```
var a = 2;

function foo() { // <-- insert this

    var a = 3;
    console.log( a ); // 3

} // <-- and this
foo(); // <-- and this

console.log( a ); // 2
```

While this technique works, it is not necessarily very ideal. There are a few problems it introduces. The first is that we have to declare a named-function foo(), which means that the identifier name foo itself "pollutes" the enclosing scope (global, in this case). We also have to explicitly call the function by name (foo()) so that the wrapped code actually executes.

It would be more ideal if the function didn't need a name (or, rather, the name didn't pollute the enclosing scope), and if the function could automatically be executed.

Fortunately, JavaScript offers a solution to both problems.

```
var a = 2;

(function foo(){ // <-- insert this

    var a = 3;
    console.log( a ); // 3
```

```
})(); // <-- and this

console.log( a ); // 2
```

Let's break down what's happening here.

First, notice that the wrapping function statement starts with (func
tion... as opposed to just function.... While this may seem like a minor
detail, it's actually a major change. Instead of treating the function as
a standard declaration, the function is treated as a function-
expression.

 The easiest way to distinguish declaration vs. expression is the
position of the word function in the statement (not just a line,
but a distinct statement). If function is the very first thing in
the statement, then it's a function declaration. Otherwise, it's a
function expression.

The key difference we can observe here between a function declaration
and a function expression relates to where its name is bound as an
identifier.

Compare the previous two snippets. In the first snippet, the name foo
is bound in the enclosing scope, and we call it directly with foo(). In
the second snippet, the name foo is not bound in the enclosing scope,
but instead is bound only inside of its own function.

In other words, (function foo(){ .. }) as an expression means the
identifier foo is found *only* in the scope where the .. indicates, not in
the outer scope. Hiding the name foo inside itself means it does not
pollute the enclosing scope unnecessarily.

Anonymous Versus Named

You are probably most familiar with function expressions as callback
parameters, such as:

```
setTimeout( function(){
    console.log("I waited 1 second!");
}, 1000 );
```

This is called an *anonymous function expression*, because function()
... has no name identifier on it. Function expressions can be anonymous, but function declarations cannot omit the name—that would
be illegal JS grammar.

Anonymous function expressions are quick and easy to type, and many libraries and tools tend to encourage this idiomatic style of code. However, they have several drawbacks to consider:

1. Anonymous functions have no useful name to display in stack traces, which can make debugging more difficult.

2. Without a name, if the function needs to refer to itself, for recursion, etc., the *deprecated* arguments.callee reference is unfortunately required. Another example of needing to self-reference is when an event handler function wants to unbind itself after it fires.

3. Anonymous functions omit a name, which is often helpful in providing more readable/understandable code. A descriptive name helps self-document the code in question.

Inline function expressions are powerful and useful—the question of anonymous versus named doesn't detract from that. Providing a name for your function expression quite effectively addresses all these drawbacks, but has no tangible downsides. The best practice is to always name your function expressions:

```
setTimeout( function timeoutHandler(){ // <-- Look, I have a
                                       // name!
    console.log( "I waited 1 second!" );
}, 1000 );
```

Invoking Function Expressions Immediately

```
var a = 2;

(function foo(){

    var a = 3;
    console.log( a ); // 3

})();

console.log( a ); // 2
```

Now that we have a function as an expression by virtue of wrapping it in a ( ) pair, we can execute that function by adding another () on the end, like (function foo(){ .. })(). The first enclosing ( ) pair makes the function an expression, and the second () executes the function.

This pattern is so common, a few years ago the community agreed on a term for it: *IIFE*, which stands for immediately invoked function expression.

Of course, IIFEs don't need names, necessarily—the most common form of IIFE is to use an anonymous function expression. While certainly less common, naming an IIFE has all the aforementioned benefits over anonymous function expressions, so it's a good practice to adopt.

```
var a = 2;

(function IIFE(){

    var a = 3;
    console.log( a ); // 3

})();

console.log( a ); // 2
```

There's a slight variation on the traditional IIFE form, which some prefer: `(function(){ .. }())`. Look closely to see the difference. In the first form, the function expression is wrapped in ( ), and then the invoking ( ) pair is on the outside right after it. In the second form, the invoking ( ) pair is moved to the inside of the outer ( ) wrapping pair.

These two forms are identical in functionality. *It's purely a stylistic choice which you prefer.*

Another variation on IIFEs that is quite common is to use the fact that they are, in fact, just function calls, and pass in argument(s).

For instance:

```
var a = 2;

(function IIFE( global ){

    var a = 3;
    console.log( a ); // 3
    console.log( global.a ); // 2

})( window );

console.log( a ); // 2
```

We pass in the `window` object reference, but we name the parameter `global`, so that we have a clear stylistic delineation for global versus nonglobal references. Of course, you can pass in anything from an enclosing scope you want, and you can name the parameter(s) anything that suits you. This is mostly just stylistic choice.

Another application of this pattern addresses the (minor niche) concern that the default undefined identifier might have its value incorrectly overwritten, causing unexpected results. By naming a parameter undefined, but not passing any value for that argument, we can guarantee that the undefined identifier is in fact the undefined value in a block of code:

```
undefined = true; // setting a land-mine for other code! avoid!

(function IIFE( undefined ){

    var a;
    if (a === undefined) {
        console.log( "Undefined is safe here!" );
    }

})();
```

Still another variation of the IIFE inverts the order of things, where the function to execute is given second, *after* the invocation and parameters to pass to it. This pattern is used in the UMD (Universal Module Definition) project. Some people find it a little cleaner to understand, though it is slightly more verbose.

```
var a = 2;

(function IIFE( def ){
    def( window );
})(function def( global ){

    var a = 3;
    console.log( a ); // 3
    console.log( global.a ); // 2

});
```

The def function expression is defined in the second-half of the snippet, and then passed as a parameter (also called def) to the IIFE function defined in the first half of the snippet. Finally, the parameter def (the function) is invoked, passing window in as the global parameter.

Blocks as Scopes

While functions are the most common unit of scope, and certainly the most widespread of the design approaches in the majority of JS in circulation, other units of scope are possible, and the usage of these other scope units can lead to even better, cleaner to maintain code.

Many languages other than JavaScript support block scope, and so developers from those languages are accustomed to the mindset, whereas those who've primarily only worked in JavaScript may find the concept slightly foreign.

But even if you've never written a single line of code in block-scoped fashion, you are still probably familiar with this extremely common idiom in JavaScript:

```
for (var i=0; i<10; i++) {
    console.log( i );
}
```

We declare the variable i directly inside the for loop head, most likely because our *intent* is to use i only within the context of that for loop, and essentially ignore the fact that the variable actually scopes itself to the enclosing scope (function or global).

That's what block-scoping is all about. Declaring variables as close as possible, as local as possible, to where they will be used. Another example:

```
var foo = true;

if (foo) {
    var bar = foo * 2;
    bar = something( bar );
    console.log( bar );
}
```

We are using a bar variable only in the context of the if statement, so it makes a kind of sense that we would declare it inside the if block. However, where we declare variables is not relevant when using var, because they will always belong to the enclosing scope. This snippet is essentially fake block-scoping, for stylistic reasons, and relying on self-enforcement not to accidentally use bar in another place in that scope.

Block scope is a tool to extend the earlier Principle of Least *Privilege* from hiding information in functions to hiding information in blocks of our code.

Consider the `for` loop example again:

```
for (var i=0; i<10; i++) {
    console.log( i );
}
```

Why pollute the entire scope of a function with the `i` variable that is only going to be (or only *should be*, at least) used for the `for` loop?

But more important, developers may prefer to *check* themselves against accidentally (re)using variables outside of their intended purpose, such being issued an error about an unknown variable if you try to use it in the wrong place. Block-scoping (if it were possible) for the `i` variable would make `i` available only for the `for` loop, causing an error if `i` is accessed elsewhere in the function. This helps ensure variables are not reused in confusing or hard-to-maintain ways.

But, the sad reality is that, on the surface, JavaScript has no facility for block scope.

That is, until you dig a little further.

with

We learned about `with` in Chapter 2. While it is a frowned-upon construct, it *is* an example of (a form of) block scope, in that the scope that is created from the object only exists for the lifetime of that `with` statement, and not in the enclosing scope.

try/catch

It's a *very* little known fact that JavaScript in ES3 specified the variable declaration in the `catch` clause of a `try/catch` to be block-scoped to the `catch` block.

For instance:

```
try {
    undefined(); // illegal operation to force an exception!
}
catch (err) {
    console.log( err ); // works!
}

console.log( err ); // ReferenceError: `err` not found
```

As you can see, `err` exists only in the `catch` clause, and throws an error when you try to reference it elsewhere.

While this behavior has been specified and true of practically all standard JS environments (except perhaps old IE), many linters seem to still complain if you have two or more catch clauses in the same scope that each declare their error variable with the same identifier name. This is not actually a re-definition, since the variables are safely block-scoped, but the linters still seem to, annoyingly, complain about this fact.

To avoid these unnecessary warnings, some devs will name their catch variables err1, err2, etc. Other devs will simply turn off the linting check for duplicate variable names.

The block-scoping nature of catch may seem like a useless academic fact, but see Appendix B for more information on just how useful it might be.

let

Thus far, we've seen that JavaScript only has some strange niche behaviors that expose block scope functionality. If that were all we had, and *it was* for many, many years, then block scoping would not be terribly useful to the JavaScript developer.

Fortunately, ES6 changes that, and introduces a new keyword let, which sits alongside var as another way to declare variables.

The let keyword attaches the variable declaration to the scope of whatever block (commonly a { .. } pair) it's contained in. In other words, let implicitly hijacks any block's scope for its variable declaration.

```
var foo = true;

if (foo) {
    let bar = foo * 2;
    bar = something( bar );
    console.log( bar );
}

console.log( bar ); // ReferenceError
```

Using let to attach a variable to an existing block is somewhat implicit. It can confuse if you're not paying close attention to which blocks have variables scoped to them and are in the habit of moving blocks around, wrapping them in other blocks, etc., as you develop and evolve code.

Creating explicit blocks for block-scoping can address some of these concerns, making it more obvious where variables are attached and not. Usually, explicit code is preferable over implicit or subtle code. This explicit block-scoping style is easy to achieve and fits more naturally with how block-scoping works in other languages:

```
var foo = true;

if (foo) {
    { // <-- explicit block
        let bar = foo * 2;
        bar = something( bar );
        console.log( bar );
    }
}

console.log( bar ); // ReferenceError
```

We can create an arbitrary block for `let` to bind to by simply including a `{ .. }` pair anywhere a statement is valid grammar. In this case, we've made an explicit block *inside* the `if` statement, which may be easier as a whole block to move around later in refactoring, without affecting the position and semantics of the enclosing `if` statment.

 For another way to express explicit block scopes, see Appendix B.

In Chapter 4, we will address hoisting, which talks about declarations being taken as existing for the entire scope in which they occur.

However, declarations made with `let` will not hoist to the entire scope of the block they appear in. Such declarations will not observably "exist" in the block until the declaration statement.

```
{
    console.log( bar ); // ReferenceError!
    let bar = 2;
}
```

Garbage collection

Another reason block-scoping is useful relates to closures and garbage collection to reclaim memory. We'll briefly illustrate here, but the closure mechanism is explained in detail in Chapter 5.

Consider:

```
function process(data) {
    // do something interesting
}

var someReallyBigData = { .. };

process( someReallyBigData );

var btn = document.getElementById( "my_button" );

btn.addEventListener( "click", function click(evt){
    console.log("button clicked");
}, /*capturingPhase=*/false );
```

The `click` function click handler callback doesn't *need* the `someReal
lyBigData` variable at all. That means, theoretically, after `pro
cess(..)` runs, the big memory-heavy data structure could be garbage
collected. However, it's quite likely (though implementation depen-
dent) that the JS engine will still have to keep the structure around,
since the `click` function has a closure over the entire scope.

Block-scoping can address this concern, making it clearer to the engine that it does not need to keep `someReallyBigData` around:

```
function process(data) {
    // do something interesting
}

// anything declared inside this block can go away after!
{
    let someReallyBigData = { .. };

    process( someReallyBigData );
}

var btn = document.getElementById( "my_button" );

btn.addEventListener( "click", function click(evt){
    console.log("button clicked");
}, /*capturingPhase=*/false );
```

Declaring explicit blocks for variables to locally bind to is a powerful
tool that you can add to your code toolbox.

let loops

A particular case where `let` shines is in the `for` loop case as we discussed previously.

```
for (let i=0; i<10; i++) {
    console.log( i );
}

console.log( i ); // ReferenceError
```

Not only does let in the for loop header bind the i to the for loop body, but in fact, it *rebinds it* to each *iteration* of the loop, making sure to reassign it the value from the end of the previous loop iteration.

Here's another way of illustrating the per-iteration binding behavior that occurs:

```
{
    let j;
    for (j=0; j<10; j++) {
        let i = j; // re-bound for each iteration!
        console.log( i );
    }
}
```

The reason why this per-iteration binding is interesting will become clear in Chapter 5 when we discuss closures.

Because let declarations attach to arbitrary blocks rather than to the enclosing function's scope (or global), there can be gotchas where existing code has a hidden reliance on function-scoped var declarations, and replacing the var with let may require additional care when refactoring code.

Consider:

```
var foo = true, baz = 10;

if (foo) {
    var bar = 3;

    if (baz > bar) {
        console.log( baz );
    }

    // ...
}
```

This code is fairly easily refactored as:

```
var foo = true, baz = 10;

if (foo) {
    var bar = 3;
```

```
        // ...
    }

    if (baz > bar) {
        console.log( baz );
    }
```

But, be careful of such changes when using block-scoped variables:

```
    var foo = true, baz = 10;

    if (foo) {
        let bar = 3;

        if (baz > bar) { // <-- don't forget `bar` when moving!
            console.log( baz );
        }
    }
```

See Appendix B for an alternate (more explicit) style of block-scoping that may provide easier to maintain/refactor code that's more robust to these scenarios.

const

In addition to let, ES6 introduces const, which also creates a block-scoped variable, but whose value is fixed (constant). Any attempt to change that value at a later time results in an error.

```
    var foo = true;

    if (foo) {
        var a = 2;
        const b = 3; // block-scoped to the containing `if`

        a = 3; // just fine!
        b = 4; // error!
    }

    console.log( a ); // 3
    console.log( b ); // ReferenceError!
```

Review

Functions are the most common unit of scope in JavaScript. Variables and functions that are declared inside another function are essentially "hidden" from any of the enclosing scopes, which is an intentional design principle of good software.

But functions are by no means the only unit of scope. Block scope refers to the idea that variables and functions can belong to an arbitrary block (generally, any { .. } pair) of code, rather than only to the enclosing function.

Starting with ES3, the try/catch structure has block scope in the catch clause.

In ES6, the let keyword (a cousin to the var keyword) is introduced to allow declarations of variables in any arbitrary block of code. if (..) { let a = 2; } will declare a variable a that essentially hijacks the scope of the if's { .. } block and attaches itself there.

Though some seem to believe so, block scope should not be taken as an outright replacement of var function scope. Both functionalities co-exist, and developers can and should use both function-scope and block-scope techniques where respectively appropriate to produce better, more readable/maintainable code.

CHAPTER 4

Hoisting

By now, you should be fairly comfortable with the idea of scope, and how variables are attached to different levels of scope depending on where and how they are declared. Both function scope and block scope behave by the same rules in this regard: any variable declared within a scope is attached to that scope.

But there's a subtle detail of how scope attachment works with declarations that appear in various locations within a scope, and that detail is what we will examine here.

Chicken or the Egg?

There's a temptation to think that all of the code you see in a JavaScript program is interpreted line-by-line, top-down in order, as the program executes. While that is substantially true, there's one part of that assumption that can lead to incorrect thinking about your program.

Consider this code:

```
a = 2;

var a;

console.log( a );
```

What do you expect to be printed in the `console.log(..)` statement?

Many developers would expect `undefined`, since the `var a` statement comes after the `a = 2`, and it would seem natural to assume that the variable is redefined, and thus assigned the default `undefined`. However, the output will be 2.

Consider another piece of code:

```
console.log( a );

var a = 2;
```

You might be tempted to assume that, since the previous snippet exhibited some less-than-top-down looking behavior, perhaps in this snippet, 2 will also be printed. Others may think that since the a variable is used before it is declared, this must result in a `ReferenceError` being thrown.

Unfortunately, both guesses are incorrect. `undefined` is the output.

So, what's going on here? It would appear we have a chicken-and-the-egg question. Which comes first, the declaration ("egg"), or the assignment ("chicken")?

The Compiler Strikes Again

To answer this question, we need to refer back to Chapter 1, and our discussion of compilers. Recall that the engine actually will compile your JavaScript code before it interprets it. Part of the compilation phase was to find and associate all declarations with their appropriate scopes. Chapter 2 showed us that this is the heart of lexical scope.

So, the best way to think about things is that all declarations, both variables and functions, are processed first, before any part of your code is executed.

When you see `var a = 2;`, you probably think of that as one statement. But JavaScript actually thinks of it as two statements: `var a;` and `a = 2;`. The first statement, the declaration, is processed during the compilation phase. The second statement, the assignment, is left *in place* for the execution phase.

Our first snippet then should be thought of as being handled like this:

```
var a;

a = 2;

console.log( a );
```

...where the first part is the compilation and the second part is the execution.

Similarly, our second snippet is actually processed as:

```
var a;

console.log( a );

a = 2;
```

So, one way of thinking, sort of metaphorically, about this process, is that variable and function declarations are "moved" from where they appear in the flow of the code to the top of the code. This gives rise to the name *hoisting*.

In other words, *the egg (declaration) comes before the chicken (assignment)*.

 Only the declarations themselves are hoisted, while any assignments or other executable logic are left *in place*. If hoisting were to re-arrange the executable logic of our code, that could wreak havoc.

```
foo();

function foo() {
    console.log( a ); // undefined

    var a = 2;
}
```

The function foo's declaration (which in this case *includes* the implied value of it as an actual function) is hoisted, such that the call on the first line is able to execute.

It's also important to note that hoisting is *per-scope*. So while our previous snippets were simplified in that they only included global scope, the foo(..) function we are now examining itself exhibits that var a is hoisted to the top of foo(..) (not, obviously, to the top of the program). So the program can perhaps be more accurately interpreted like this:

```
function foo() {
    var a;

    console.log( a ); // undefined

    a = 2;
```

```
}

foo();
```

Function declarations are hoisted, as we just saw. But function expressions are not.

```
foo(); // not ReferenceError, but TypeError!

var foo = function bar() {
    // ...
};
```

The variable identifier foo is hoisted and attached to the enclosing
scope (global) of this program, so foo() doesn't fail as a ReferenceEr
ror. But foo has no value yet (as it would if it had been a true function
declaration instead of expression). So, foo() is attempting to invoke
the undefined value, which is a TypeError illegal operation.

Also recall that even though it's a named function expression, the name
identifier is not available in the enclosing scope:

```
foo(); // TypeError
bar(); // ReferenceError

var foo = function bar() {
    // ...
};
```

This snippet is more accurately interpreted (with hoisting) as:

```
var foo;

foo(); // TypeError
bar(); // ReferenceError

foo = function() {
    var bar = ...self...
    // ...
}
```

Functions First

Both function declarations and variable declarations are hoisted. But
a subtle detail (that *can* show up in code with multiple "duplicate"
declarations) is that functions are hoisted first, and then variables.

Consider:

```
foo(); // 1

var foo;

function foo() {
    console.log( 1 );
}

foo = function() {
    console.log( 2 );
};
```

1 is printed instead of 2! This snippet is interpreted by the *Engine* as:

```
function foo() {
    console.log( 1 );
}

foo(); // 1

foo = function() {
    console.log( 2 );
};
```

Notice that var foo was the duplicate (and thus ignored) declaration, even though it came before the function foo()... declaration, because function declarations are hoisted before normal variables.

While multiple/duplicate var declarations are effectively ignored, subsequent function declarations *do* override previous ones.

```
foo(); // 3

function foo() {
    console.log( 1 );
}

var foo = function() {
    console.log( 2 );
};

function foo() {
    console.log( 3 );
}
```

While this all may sound like nothing more than interesting academic trivia, it highlights the fact that duplicate definitions in the same scope are a really bad idea and will often lead to confusing results.

Function declarations that appear inside of normal blocks typically hoist to the enclosing scope, rather than being conditional as this code implies:

```
foo(); // "b"

var a = true;
if (a) {
    function foo() { console.log("a"); }
}
else {
    function foo() { console.log("b"); }
}
```

However, it's important to note that this behavior is not reliable and is subject to change in future versions of JavaScript, so it's probably best to avoid declaring functions in blocks.

Review

We can be tempted to look at var a = 2; as one statement, but the JavaScript engine does not see it that way. It sees var a and a = 2 as two separate statements, the first one a compiler-phase task, and the second one an execution-phase task.

What this leads to is that all declarations in a scope, regardless of where they appear, are processed *first* before the code itself is executed. You can visualize this as declarations (variables and functions) being "moved" to the top of their respective scopes, which we call *hoisting*.

Declarations themselves are hoisted, but assignments, even assignments of function expressions, are *not* hoisted.

Be careful about duplicate declarations, especially mixed between normal var declarations and function declarations—peril awaits if you do!

Scope Closure

We arrive at this point with hopefully a very healthy, solid understanding of how scope works.

We turn our attention to an incredibly important, but persistently elusive, *almost mythological*, part of the language: *closure*. If you have followed our discussion of lexical scope thus far, the payoff is that closure is going to be, largely, anticlimactic, almost self-obvious. *There's a man behind the wizard's curtain, and we're about to see him.* No, his name is not Crockford!

If however you have nagging questions about lexical scope, now would be a good time to go back and review Chapter 2 before proceeding.

Enlightenment

For those who are somewhat experienced in JavaScript but have perhaps never fully grasped the concept of closures, understanding closure can seem like a special nirvana that one must strive and sacrifice to attain.

I recall years back when I had a firm grasp on JavaScript but had no idea what closure was. The hint that there was this other side to the language, one that promised even more capability than I already possessed, but it teased and taunted me. I remember reading through the source code of early frameworks trying to understand how it actually worked. I remember the first time something of the "module pattern" began to emerge in my mind. I remember the aha! moments quite vividly.

What I didn't know back then, what took me years to understand, and what I hope to impart to you presently, is this secret: *closure is all around you in JavaScript, you just have to recognize and embrace it.* Closures are not a special opt-in tool that you must learn new syntax and patterns for. No, closures are not even a weapon that you must learn to wield and master as Luke trained in the Force.

Closures happen as a result of writing code that relies on lexical scope. They just happen. You do not even really have to intentionally create closures to take advantage of them. Closures are created and used for you all over your code. What you are *missing* is the proper mental context to recognize, embrace, and leverage closures for your own will.

The enlightenment moment should be: oh, closures are already occurring all over my code, I can finally see them now. Understanding closures is like when Neo sees the Matrix for the first time.

Nitty Gritty

OK, enough hyperbole and shameless movie references.

Here's a down-and-dirty definition of what you need to know to understand and recognize closures:

> Closure is when a function is able to remember and access its lexical scope even when that function is executing outside its lexical scope.

Let's jump into some code to illustrate that definition.

```
function foo() {
    var a = 2;

    function bar() {
        console.log( a ); // 2
    }

    bar();
}

foo();
```

This code should look familiar from our discussions of nested scope. Function bar() has *access* to the variable a in the outer enclosing scope because of lexical scope look-up rules (in this case, it's an RHS reference look-up).

Is this closure?

Well, technically...*perhaps*. But by our what-you-need-to-know definition above...*not exactly*. I think the most accurate way to explain bar() referencing a is via lexical scope look-up rules, and those rules are *only* (an important!) *part* of what closure is.

From a purely academic perspective, what is said of the above snippet is that the function bar() has a *closure* over the scope of foo() (and indeed, even over the rest of the scopes it has access to, such as the global scope in our case). Put slightly differently, it's said that bar() closes over the scope of foo(). Why? Because bar() appears nested inside of foo(). Plain and simple.

But, closure defined in this way is not directly *observable*, nor do we see closure *exercised* in that snippet. We clearly see lexical scope, but closure remains sort of a mysterious shifting shadow behind the code.

Let us then consider code that brings closure into full light:

```
function foo() {
    var a = 2;

    function bar() {
        console.log( a );
    }

    return bar;
}

var baz = foo();

baz(); // 2 -- Whoa, closure was just observed, man.
```

The function bar() has lexical scope access to the inner scope of foo(). But then, we take bar(), the function itself, and pass it *as* a value. In this case, we return the function object itself that bar references.

After we execute foo(), we assign the value it returned (our inner bar() function) to a variable called baz, and then we actually invoke baz(), which of course is invoking our inner function bar(), just by a different identifier reference.

bar() is executed, for sure. But in this case, it's executed *outside* of its declared lexical scope.

After foo() executed, normally we would expect that the entirety of the inner scope of foo() would go away, because we know that the engine employs a garbage collector that comes along and frees up memory once it's no longer in use. Since it would appear that the contents of foo() are no longer in use, it would seem natural that they should be considered *gone*.

But the "magic" of closures does not let this happen. That inner scope is in fact *still* in use, and thus does not go away. Who's using it? The function bar() itself.

By virtue of where it was declared, bar() has a lexical scope closure over that inner scope of foo(), which keeps that scope alive for bar() to reference at any later time.

bar() still has a reference to that scope, and that reference is called closure.

So, a few microseconds later, when the variable baz is invoked (invoking the inner function we initially labeled bar), it duly has *access* to author-time lexical scope, so it can access the variable a just as we'd expect.

The function is being invoked well outside of its author-time lexical scope. Closure lets the function continue to access the lexical scope it was defined in at author time.

Of course, any of the various ways that functions can be *passed around* as values, and indeed invoked in other locations, are all examples of observing/exercising closure.

```
function foo() {
    var a = 2;

    function baz() {
        console.log( a ); // 2
    }

    bar( baz );
}

function bar(fn) {
    fn(); // look ma, I saw closure!
}
```

We pass the inner function baz over to bar, and call that inner function (labeled fn now), and when we do, its closure over the inner scope of foo() is observed by accessing a.

These passings-around of functions can be indirect, too.

```
var fn;

function foo() {
    var a = 2;

    function baz() {
        console.log( a );
    }

    fn = baz; // assign baz to global variable
}

function bar() {
    fn(); // look ma, I saw closure!
}

foo();

bar(); // 2
```

Whatever facility we use to *transport* an inner function outside of its lexical scope, it will maintain a scope reference to where it was originally declared, and wherever we execute him, that closure will be exercised.

Now I Can See

The previous code snippets are somewhat academic and artifically constructed to illustrate *using closure*. But I promised you something more than just a cool new toy. I promised that closure was something all around you in your existing code. Let us now *see* that truth.

```
function wait(message) {

    setTimeout( function timer(){
        console.log( message );
    }, 1000 );

}

wait( "Hello, closure!" );
```

We take an inner function (named `timer`) and pass it to `setTime out(..)`. But `timer` has a scope closure over the scope of `wait(..)`, indeed keeping and using a reference to the variable `message`.

A thousand milliseconds after we have executed `wait(..)`, and its inner scope should otherwise be long gone, that anonymous function still has closure over that scope.

Deep down in the guts of the engine, the built-in utility `setTimeout(..)` has reference to some parameter, probably called `fn` or `func` or something like that. Engine goes to invoke that function, which is invoking our inner `timer` function, and the lexical scope reference is still intact.

Closure.

Or, if you're of the jQuery persuasion (or any JS framework, for that matter):

```
function setupBot(name,selector) {
    $( selector ).click( function activator(){
        console.log( "Activating: " + name );
    } );
}

setupBot( "Closure Bot 1", "#bot_1" );
setupBot( "Closure Bot 2", "#bot_2" );
```

I am not sure what kind of code you write, but I regularly write code that is responsible for controlling an entire global drone army of closure bots, so this is totally realistic!

(Some) joking aside, essentially *whenever* and *wherever* you treat functions (that access their own respective lexical scopes) as first-class values and pass them around, you are likely to see those functions exercising closure. Be that timers, event handlers, Ajax requests, cross-window messaging, web workers, or any of the other asynchronous (or synchronous!) tasks, when you pass in a *callback function*, get ready to sling some closure around!

 Chapter 3 introduced the IIFE pattern. While it is often said that IIFE (alone) is an example of observed closure, I would somewhat disagree, by our previous definition.

```
var a = 2;

(function IIFE(){
    console.log( a );
})();
```

This code works, but it's not strictly an observation of closure. Why? Because the function (which we named IIFE here) is not executed outside its lexical scope. It's still invoked right there in the same scope as it was declared (then enclosing/global scope that also holds a). a is found via normal lexical scope look-up, not really via closure.

While closure might technically be happening at declaration time, it is *not* strictly observable, and so, as they say, *it's a tree falling in the forest with no one around to hear it.*

Though an IIFE is not *itself* an example of observed closure, it absolutely creates scope, and it's one of the most common tools we use to create scope which can be closed over. So IIFEs are indeed heavily related to closure, even if not exercising closure themselves.

Put this book down right now, dear reader. I have a task for you. Go open up some of your recent JavaScript code. Look for your functions-as-values and identify where you are already using closure and maybe didn't even know it before.

I'll wait.

Now you see!

Loops and Closure

The most common canonical example used to illustrate closure involves the humble for loop.

```
for (var i=1; i<=5; i++) {
    setTimeout( function timer(){
        console.log( i );
    }, i*1000 );
}
```

 Linters often complain when you put functions inside of loops, because the mistakes of not understanding closure are *so common among developers.* We explain how to do so properly here, leveraging the full power of closure. But that subtlety is often lost on linters, and they will complain regardless, assuming you don't *actually* know what you're doing.

The spirit of this code snippet is that we would normally *expect* for the behavior to be that the numbers 1, 2,…5 would be printed out, one at a time, one per second, respectively.

In fact, if you run this code, you get 6 printed out five times, at the one-second intervals.

Huh?

First, let's explain where 6 comes from. The terminating condition of the loop is when i is *not* <=5. The first time that's the case is when i is 6. So, the output is reflecting the final value of the i after the loop terminates.

This actually seems obvious on second glance. The timeout function callbacks are all running well after the completion of the loop. In fact, as timers go, even if it was setTimeout(.., 0) on each iteration, all those function callbacks would still run strictly after the completion of the loop, and thus print 6 each time.

But there's a deeper question at play here. What's *missing* from our code to actually have it behave as we semantically have implied?

What's missing is that we are trying to *imply* that each iteration of the loop "captures" its own copy of i, at the time of the iteration. But, the way scope works, all five of those functions, though they are defined separately in each loop iteration, *are closed over the same shared global scope*, which has, in fact, only one i in it.

Put that way, *of course* all functions share a reference to the same i. Something about the loop structure tends to confuse us into thinking there's something else more sophisticated at work. There is not. There's no difference than if each of the five timeout callbacks were just declared one right after the other, with no loop at all.

OK, so, back to our burning question. What's missing? We need more closured scope. Specifically, we need a new closured scope for each iteration of the loop.

We learned in Chapter 3 that the IIFE creates scope by declaring a function and immediately executing it.

Let's try:

```
for (var i=1; i<=5; i++) {
    (function(){
        setTimeout( function timer(){
            console.log( i );
        }, i*1000 );
    })();
}
```

Does that work? Try it. Again, I'll wait.

I'll end the suspense for you. *Nope.* But why? We now obviously have more lexical scope. Each timeout function callback is indeed closing over its own per-iteration scope created respectively by each IIFE.

It's not enough to have a scope to close over *if that scope is empty.* Look closely. Our IIFE is just an empty do-nothing scope. It needs *something* in it to be useful to us.

It needs its own variable, with a copy of the i value at each iteration.

```
for (var i=1; i<=5; i++) {
    (function(){
        var j = i;
        setTimeout( function timer(){
            console.log( j );
        }, j*1000 );
    })();
}
```

Eureka! It works!

A slight variation some prefer is:

```
for (var i=1; i<=5; i++) {
    (function(j){
        setTimeout( function timer(){
            console.log( j );
        }, j*1000 );
    })( i );
}
```

Of course, since these IIFEs are just functions, we can pass in i, and we can call it j if we prefer, or we can even call it i again. Either way, the code works now.

The use of an IIFE inside each iteration created a new scope for each iteration, which gave our timeout function callbacks the opportunity to close over a new scope for each iteration, one which had a variable with the right per-iteration value in it for us to access.

Problem solved!

Block Scoping Revisited

Look carefully at our analysis of the previous solution. We used an IIFE to create new scope per-iteration. In other words, we actually *needed* a per-iteration *block scope*. Chapter 3 showed us the let declaration, which hijacks a block and declares a variable right there in the block.

It essentially turns a block into a scope that we can close over. So, the following awesome code just works:

```
for (var i=1; i<=5; i++) {
    let j = i; // yay, block-scope for closure!
    setTimeout( function timer(){
        console.log( j );
    }, j*1000 );
}
```

But, that's not all! (in my best Bob Barker voice). There's a special behavior defined for `let` declarations used in the head of a `for` loop. This behavior says that the variable will be declared not just once for the loop, **but each iteration**. And, it will, helpfully, be initialized at each subsequent iteration with the value from the end of the previous iteration.

```
for (let i=1; i<=5; i++) {
    setTimeout( function timer(){
        console.log( i );
    }, i*1000 );
}
```

How cool is that? Block scoping and closure working hand-in-hand, solving all the world's problems. I don't know about you, but that makes me a happy JavaScripter.

Modules

There are other code patterns that leverage the power of closure but that do not on the surface appear to be about callbacks. Let's examine the most powerful of them: *the module.*

```
function foo() {
    var something = "cool";
    var another = [1, 2, 3];

    function doSomething() {
        console.log( something );
    }

    function doAnother() {
        console.log( another.join( " ! " ) );
    }
}
```

As this code stands right now, there's no observable closure going on. We simply have some private data variables something and another, and a couple of inner functions doSomething() and doAnother(), which both have lexical scope (and thus closure!) over the inner scope of foo().

But now consider:

```
function CoolModule() {
    var something = "cool";
    var another = [1, 2, 3];

    function doSomething() {
        console.log( something );
    }

    function doAnother() {
        console.log( another.join( " ! " ) );
    }

    return {
        doSomething: doSomething,
        doAnother: doAnother
    };
}

var foo = CoolModule();

foo.doSomething(); // cool
foo.doAnother(); // 1 ! 2 ! 3
```

This is the pattern in JavaScript we call *module*. The most common way of implementing the module pattern is often called *revealing module*, and it's the variation we present here.

Let's examine some things about this code.

First, CoolModule() is just a function, but it *has to be invoked* for there to be a module instance created. Without the execution of the outer function, the creation of the inner scope and the closures would not occur.

Second, the CoolModule() function returns an object, denoted by the object-literal syntax { key: value, ... }. The object we return has references on it to our inner functions, but *not* to our inner data variables. We keep those hidden and private. It's appropriate to think of this object return value as essentially a *public API for our module*.

This object return value is ultimately assigned to the outer variable foo, and then we can access those property methods on the API, like foo.doSomething().

It is not required that we return an actual object (literal) from our module. We could just return back an inner function directly. jQuery is actually a good example of this. The jQuery and $ identifiers are the public API for the jQuery module, but they are, themselves, just functions (which can themselves have properties, since all functions are objects).

The doSomething() and doAnother() functions have closure over the inner scope of the module instance (arrived at by actually invoking CoolModule()). When we transport those functions outside of the lexical scope, by way of property references on the object we return, we have now set up a condition by which closure can be observed and exercised.

To state it more simply, there are two requirements for the module pattern to be exercised:

1. There must be an outer enclosing function, and it must be invoked at least once (each time creates a new module instance).

2. The enclosing function must return back at least one inner function, so that this inner function has closure over the private scope, and can access and/or modify that private state.

An object with a function property on it alone is not *really* a module. An object that is returned from a function invocation that only has data properties on it and no closured functions is not *really* a module, in the observable sense.

The previous code snippet shows a standalone module creator called CoolModule(), which can be invoked any number of times, each time creating a new module instance. A slight variation on this pattern is when you only care to have one instance, a singleton of sorts:

```
var foo = (function CoolModule() {
    var something = "cool";
    var another = [1, 2, 3];

    function doSomething() {
        console.log( something );
    }
```

```
    function doAnother() {
        console.log( another.join( " ! " ) );
    }

    return {
        doSomething: doSomething,
        doAnother: doAnother
    };
})();

foo.doSomething(); // cool
foo.doAnother(); // 1 ! 2 ! 3
```

Here, we turned our module function into an IIFE (see Chapter 3), and we *immediately* invoked it and assigned its return value directly to our single module instance identifier foo.

Modules are just functions, so they can receive parameters:

```
function CoolModule(id) {
    function identify() {
        console.log( id );
    }

    return {
        identify: identify
    };
}

var foo1 = CoolModule( "foo 1" );
var foo2 = CoolModule( "foo 2" );

foo1.identify(); // "foo 1"
foo2.identify(); // "foo 2"
```

Another slight but powerful variation on the module pattern is to name the object you are returning as your public API:

```
var foo = (function CoolModule(id) {
    function change() {
        // modifying the public API
        publicAPI.identify = identify2;
    }

    function identify1() {
        console.log( id );
    }

    function identify2() {
        console.log( id.toUpperCase() );
    }
```

```
    var publicAPI = {
        change: change,
        identify: identify1
    };

    return publicAPI;
})( "foo module" );

foo.identify(); // foo module
foo.change();
foo.identify(); // FOO MODULE
```

By retaining an inner reference to the public API object inside your module instance, you can modify that module instance *from the inside*, including adding and removing methods and properties, *and* changing their values.

Modern Modules

Various module dependency loaders/managers essentially wrap up this pattern of module definition into a friendly API. Rather than examine any one particular library, let me present a *very simple* proof of concept *for illustration purposes (only)*:

```
var MyModules = (function Manager() {
    var modules = {};

    function define(name, deps, impl) {
        for (var i=0; i<deps.length; i++) {
            deps[i] = modules[deps[i]];
        }
        modules[name] = impl.apply( impl, deps );
    }

    function get(name) {
        return modules[name];
    }

    return {
        define: define,
        get: get
    };
})();
```

The key part of this code is modules[name] = impl.apply(impl, deps). This is invoking the definition wrapper function for a module (passing in any dependencies), and storing the return value, the module's API, into an internal list of modules tracked by name.

And here's how I might use it to define some modules:

```
MyModules.define( "bar", [], function(){
    function hello(who) {
        return "Let me introduce: " + who;
    }

    return {
        hello: hello
    };
} );

MyModules.define( "foo", ["bar"], function(bar){
    var hungry = "hippo";

    function awesome() {
        console.log( bar.hello( hungry ).toUpperCase() );
    }

    return {
        awesome: awesome
    };
} );

var bar = MyModules.get( "bar" );
var foo = MyModules.get( "foo" );

console.log(
    bar.hello( "hippo" )
); // Let me introduce: hippo

foo.awesome(); // LET ME INTRODUCE: HIPPO
```

Both the "foo" and "bar" modules are defined with a function that returns a public API. "foo" even receives the instance of "bar" as a dependency parameter, and can use it accordingly.

Spend some time examining these code snippets to fully understand the power of closures put to use for our own good purposes. The key take-away is that there's not really any particular "magic" to module managers. They fulfill both characteristics of the module pattern I listed above: invoking a function definition wrapper, and keeping its return value as the API for that module.

In other words, modules are just modules, even if you put a friendly wrapper tool on top of them.

Future Modules

ES6 adds first-class syntax support for the concept of modules. When loaded via the module system, ES6 treats a file as a separate module. Each module can both import other modules or specific API members, as well export their own public API members.

 Function-based modules aren't a statically recognized pattern (something the compiler knows about), so their API semantics aren't considered until runtime. That is, you can actually modify a module's API during the runtime (see earlier `publicAPI` discussion).

By contrast, ES6 module APIs are static (the APIs don't change at runtime). Since the compiler knows *that*, it can (and does!) check during (file loading and) compilation that a reference to a member of an imported module's API *actually exists*. If the API reference doesn't exist, the compiler throws an "early" error at compile time, rather than waiting for traditional dynamic runtime resolution (and errors, if any).

ES6 modules *do not* have an "inline" format, they must be defined in separate files (one per module). The browsers/engines have a default "module loader" (which is overridable, but that's well-beyond our discussion here), which synchronously loads a module file when it's imported.

Consider:

bar.js

```
function hello(who) {
    return "Let me introduce: " + who;
}

export hello;
```

foo.js

```
// import only `hello()` from the "bar" module
import hello from "bar";

var hungry = "hippo";

function awesome() {
    console.log(
        hello( hungry ).toUpperCase()
    );
```

```
    }

    export awesome;
```

baz.js

```
    // import the entire "foo" and "bar" modules
    module foo from "foo";
    module bar from "bar";

    console.log(
        bar.hello( "rhino" )
    ); // Let me introduce: rhino

    foo.awesome(); // LET ME INTRODUCE: HIPPO
```

 Separate files *foo.js* and *bar.js* would need to be created, with the contents as shown in the first two snippets, respectively. Then, your program *baz.js* would load/import those modules to use them, as shown in the third snippet.

import imports one or more members from a module's API into the current scope, each to a bound variable (hello in our case). module imports an entire module API to a bound variable (foo, bar in our case). export exports an identifier (variable, function) to the public API for the current module. These operators can be used as many times in a module's definition as is necessary.

The contents inside the *module file* are treated as if enclosed in a scope closure, just like with the function-closure modules seen earlier.

Review

Closure seems to the unenlightened like a mystical world set apart inside of JavaScript that only the few bravest souls can reach. But it's actually just a standard and almost obvious fact of how we write code in a lexically scoped environment, where functions are values and can be passed around at will.

Closure is when a function can remember and access its lexical scope even when it's invoked outside its lexical scope.

Closures can trip us up, for instance with loops, if we're not careful to recognize them and how they work. But they are also an immensely powerful tool, enabling patterns like *modules* in their various forms.

Modules require two key characteristics: 1) an outer wrapping function being invoked, to create the enclosing scope 2) the return value of the wrapping function must include reference to at least one inner function that then has closure over the private inner scope of the wrapper.

Now we can see closures all around our existing code, and we have the ability to recognize and leverage them to our own benefit!

Dynamic Scope

In Chapter 2, we talked about dynamic scope as a contrast to the lexical scope model, which is how scope works in JavaScript (and in fact, most other languages).

We will briefly examine dynamic scope, to hammer home the contrast. But, more important, dynamic scope actually is a near cousin to another mechanism (this) in JavaScript, which we cover in the *this & Object Prototypes* title of the *You Don't Know JS* book series.

As we saw in Chapter 2, lexical scope is the set of rules about how the engine can look up a variable and where it will find it. The key characteristic of lexical scope is that it is defined at author time, when the code is written (assuming you don't cheat with eval() or with).

Dynamic scope seems to imply, and for good reason, that there's a model whereby scope can be determined dynamically at runtime, rather than statically at author time. That is in fact the case. Let's illustrate via code:

```
function foo() {
    console.log( a ); // 2
}

function bar() {
    var a = 3;
    foo();
}

var a = 2;

bar();
```

Lexical scope holds that the RHS reference to a in foo() will be resolved to the global variable a, which will result in value 2 being output.

Dynamic scope, by contrast, doesn't concern itself with how and where functions and scopes are declared, but rather *where they are called from*. In other words, the scope chain is based on the call-stack, not the nesting of scopes in code.

So, if JavaScript had dynamic scope, when foo() is executed, *theoretically* the code below would instead result in 3 as the output.

```
function foo() {
    console.log( a ); // 3  (not 2!)
}

function bar() {
    var a = 3;
    foo();
}

var a = 2;

bar();
```

How can this be? Because when foo() cannot resolve the variable reference for a, instead of stepping up the nested (lexical) scope chain, it walks up the call stack, to find where foo() was *called from*. Since foo() was called from bar(), it checks the variables in scope for bar(), and finds an a there with value 3.

Strange? You're probably thinking so, at the moment.

But that's just because you've probably only ever worked on (or at least deeply considered) code that is lexically scoped. So dynamic scoping seems foreign. If you had only ever written code in a dynamically scoped language, it would seem natural, and lexical scope would be the odd ball.

To be clear, JavaScript does not, in fact, have dynamic scope. It has lexical scope. Plain and simple. But the this mechanism is kind of like dynamic scope.

The key contrast: lexical scope is write-time, whereas dynamic scope (and `this`!) are runtime. Lexical scope cares where a function was declared, but dynamic scope cares where a function was called from.

Finally, `this` cares how a function was called, which shows how closely related the `this` mechanism is to the idea of dynamic scoping. To dig more into `this`, read the *You Don't Know JS* title *this & Object Prototypes*.

Polyfilling Block Scope

In Chapter 3, we explored block scope. We saw that with and the catch clause are both tiny examples of block scope that have existed in Java-Script since at least the introduction of ES3.

But it's ES6's introduction of let that finally gives full, unfettered block scoping capability to our code. There are many exciting things, both functionally and code-stylistically, that block scope will enable.

But what if we wanted to use block scope in pre-ES6 environments?

Consider this code:

```
{
    let a = 2;
    console.log( a ); // 2
}

console.log( a ); // ReferenceError
```

This will work great in ES6 environments. But can we do so pre-ES6? catch is the answer.

```
try{throw 2}catch(a){
    console.log( a ); // 2
}

console.log( a ); // ReferenceError
```

Whoa! That's some ugly, weird looking code. We see a try/catch that appears to forcibly throw an error, but the "error" it throws is just a value 2, and then the variable declaration that receives it is in the catch(a) clause. Mind: blown.

That's right, the `catch` clause has block-scoping to it, which means it can be used as a polyfill for block scope in pre-ES6 environments.

"But", you say, "no one wants to write ugly code like that!" That's true. No one writes (some of) the code output by the CoffeeScript compiler, either. That's not the point.

The point is that tools can transpile ES6 code to work in pre-ES6 environments. You can write code using block scoping, and benefit from such functionality, and let a build-step tool take care of producing code that will actually *work* when deployed.

This is actually the preferred migration path for all (ahem, most) of ES6: to use a code transpiler to take ES6 code and produce ES5-compatible code during the transition from pre-ES6 to ES6.

Traceur

Google maintains a project called Traceur[1], which is exactly tasked with transpiling ES6 features into pre-ES6 (mostly ES5, but not all!) for general usage. The TC39 committee relies on this tool (and others) to test out the semantics of the features they specify.

What does Traceur produce from our snippet? You guessed it!

```
{
    try {
        throw undefined;
    } catch (a) {
        a = 2;
        console.log( a );
    }
}

console.log( a );
```

So, with the use of such tools, we can start taking advantage of block scope regardless of if we are targeting ES6 or not, because `try/catch` has been around (and worked this way) from ES3 days.

---

1. Google Traceur (*http://traceur-compiler.googlecode.com/git/demo/repl.html*)

Implicit Versus Explicit Blocks

In Chapter 3, we identified some potential pitfalls to code maintainability/refactorability when we introduce block scoping. Is there another way to take advantage of block scope but to reduce this downside?

Consider this alternate form of let, called the let block or let statement (contrasted with let declarations from before).

```
let (a = 2) {
    console.log( a ); // 2
}

console.log( a ); // ReferenceError
```

Instead of implicitly hijacking an existing block, the let statement creates an explicit block for its scope binding. Not only does the explicit block stand out more, and perhaps fare more robustly in code refactoring, it produces somewhat cleaner code by, grammatically, forcing all the declarations to the top of the block. This makes it easier to look at any block and know what's scoped to it and not.

As a pattern, it mirrors the approach many people take in function scoping when they manually move/hoist all their var declarations to the top of the function. The let statement puts them there at the top of the block by intent, and if you don't use let declarations strewn throughout, your block-scoping declarations are somewhat easier to identify and maintain.

But, there's a problem. The let statement form is not included in ES6. Neither does the official Traceur compiler accept that form of code.

We have two options. We can format using ES6-valid syntax and a little sprinkle of code discipline:

```
/*let*/ { let a = 2;
    console.log( a );
}

console.log( a ); // ReferenceError
```

But, tools are meant to solve our problems. So the other option is to write explicit let statement blocks, and let a tool convert them to valid, working code.

So, I built a tool called *let-er*[2] to address just this issue. *let-er* is a build-step code transpiler, but its only task is to find `let` statement forms and transpile them. It will leave alone any of the rest of your code, including any `let` declarations. You can safely use *let-er* as the first ES6 transpiler step, and then pass your code through something like Traceur if necessary.

Moreover, *let-er* has a configuration flag `--es6`, which when turned on (off by default), changes the kind of code produced. Instead of the `try/catch` ES3 polyfill hack, *let-er* would take our snippet and produce the fully ES6-compliant, non-hacky:

```
{
    let a = 2;
    console.log( a );
}

console.log( a ); // ReferenceError
```

So, you can start using *let-er* right away, and target all pre-ES6 environments, and when you only care about ES6, you can add the flag and instantly target only ES6.

And most important, you can use the more preferable and more explicit `let` statement form even though it is not an official part of any ES version (yet).

Performance

Let me add one last quick note on the performance of `try/catch`, and/or to address the question, "Why not just use an IIFE to create the scope?"

First, the performance of `try/catch` *is* slower, but there's no reasonable assumption that it *has* to be that way, or even that it *always will be* that way. Since the official TC39-approved ES6 transpiler uses `try/catch`, the Traceur team has asked Chrome to improve the performance of `try/catch`, and they are obviously motivated to do so.

Secondly, IIFE is not a fair apples-to-apples comparison with `try/catch`, because a function wrapped around any arbitrary code changes the meaning, inside of that code, of `this`, `return`, `break`, and

2. let-er on GitHub (*https://github.com/getify/let-er*)

`continue`. IIFE is not a suitable general substitute. It could only be used manually in certain cases.

The question really becomes: do you want block scoping, or not. If you do, these tools provide you that option. If not, keep using `var` and go on about your coding!

Lexical this

Though this title does not address the this mechanism in any detail, there's one ES6 topic that relates this to lexical scope in an important way, which we will quickly examine.

ES6 adds a special syntactic form of function declaration called the *arrow function*. It looks like this:

```
var foo = a => {
    console.log( a );
};

foo( 2 ); // 2
```

The so-called "fat arrow" is often mentioned as a shorthand for the *tediously verbose* (sarcasm) function keyword.

But there's something much more important going on with arrow functions that has nothing to do with saving keystrokes in your declaration. Briefly, this code suffers a problem:

```
var obj = {
    id: "awesome",
    cool: function coolFn() {
        console.log( this.id );
    }
};

var id = "not awesome"

obj.cool(); // awesome

setTimeout( obj.cool, 100 ); // not awesome
```

The problem is the loss of this binding on the cool() function. There are various ways to address that problem, but one often-repeated solution is var self = this;.

That might look like:

```
var obj = {
    count: 0,
    cool: function coolFn() {
        var self = this;

        if (self.count < 1) {
            setTimeout( function timer(){
                self.count++;
                console.log( "awesome?" );
            }, 100 );
        }
    }
};

obj.cool(); // awesome?
```

Without getting too much into the weeds here, the var self = this "solution" just ends-around the whole problem of understanding and properly using this binding, and instead falls back to something we're perhaps more comfortable with: lexical scope. self becomes just an identifier that can be resolved via lexical scope and closure, and cares not what happened to the this binding along the way.

People don't like writing verbose stuff, especially when they do it over and over again. So, a motivation of ES6 is to help alleviate these scenarios, and indeed, *fix* common idiom problems, such as this one.

The ES6 solution, the arrow function, introduces a behavior called lexical this.

```
var obj = {
    count: 0,
    cool: function coolFn() {
        if (this.count < 1) {
            setTimeout( () => { // arrow-function ftw?
                this.count++;
                console.log( "awesome?" );
            }, 100 );
        }
    }
};

obj.cool(); // awesome?
```

The short explanation is that arrow functions do not behave at all like normal functions when it comes to their this binding. They discard all the normal rules for this binding, and instead take on the this value of their immediate lexical enclosing scope, whatever it is.

So, in that snippet, the arrow function doesn't get its this unbound in some unpredictable way, it just "inherits" the this binding of the cool() function (which is correct if we invoke it as shown!).

While this makes for shorter code, my perspective is that arrow functions are really just codifying into the language syntax a common *mistake* of developers, which is to confuse and conflate this binding rules with lexical scope rules.

Put another way: why go to the trouble and verbosity of using the this style coding paradigm, only to cut it off at the knees by mixing it with lexical references. It seems natural to embrace one approach or the other for any given piece of code, and not mix them in the same piece of code.

 One other detraction from arrow functions is that they are anonymous, not named. See Chapter 3 for the reasons why anonymous functions are less desirable than named functions.

A more appropriate approach, in my perspective, to this "problem," is to use and embrace the this mechanism correctly.

```
var obj = {
    count: 0,
    cool: function coolFn() {
        if (this.count < 1) {
            setTimeout( function timer(){
                this.count++; // `this` is safe
                              // because of `bind(..)`
                console.log( "more awesome" );
            }.bind( this ), 100 ); // look, `bind()`!
        }
    }
};

obj.cool(); // more awesome
```

Whether you prefer the new lexical `this` behavior of arrow functions, or you prefer the tried-and-true `bind()`, it's important to note that arrow functions are *not* just about less typing of `function`.

They have an *intentional behavioral difference* that we should learn and understand, and if we so choose, leverage.

Now that we fully understand lexical scoping (and closure!), understanding lexical `this` should be a breeze!

Acknowledgments

I have many people to thank for making this book title and the overall series happen.

First, I must thank my wife Christen Simpson, and my two kids, Ethan and Emily, for putting up with Dad always pecking away at the computer. Even when not writing books, my obsession with JavaScript glues my eyes to the screen far more than it should. That time I borrow from my family is the reason these books can so deeply and completely explain JavaScript to you, the reader. I owe my family everything.

I'd like to thank my editors at O'Reilly, namely Simon St.Laurent and Brian MacDonald, as well as the rest of the editorial and marketing staff. They are fantastic to work with, and have been especially accommodating during this experiment into "open source" book writing, editing, and production.

Thank you to the many folks who have participated in making this book series better by providing editorial suggestions and corrections, including Shelley Powers, Tim Ferro, Evan Borden, Forrest L Norvell, Jennifer Davis, Jesse Harlin, and many others. Thank you to Shane Hudson for his fantastic Foreword.

Thank you to the countless folks in the community, including members of the TC39 committee, who have shared so much knowledge with the rest of us, and especially tolerated my incessant questions and explorations with patience and detail, including (but not limited to) John-David Dalton, Juriy "kangax" Zaytsev, Mathias Bynens, Rick Waldron, Axel Rauschmayer, Nicholas Zakas, Angus Croll, Jordan Harband, Dave Herman, Brendan Eich, Allen Wirfs-Brock, Bradley

Meck, Domenic Denicola, David Walsh, Tim Disney, Kris Kowal, Peter van der Zee, Andrea Giammarchi, Kit Cambridge, and so many others, I can't even scratch the surface.

Since the "You Don't Know JS" book series was born on Kickstarter, I also wish to thank all my (nearly) 500 generous backers, without whom this book series could not have happened: Jan Szpila, nokiko, Murali Krishnamoorthy, Ryan Joy, Craig Patchett, pdqtrader, Dale Fukami, ray hatfield, R0drigo Perez [Mx], Dan Petitt, Jack Franklin, Andrew Berry, Brian Grinstead, Rob Sutherland, Sergi Meseguer, Phillip Gourley, Mark Watson, Jeff Carouth, Alfredo Sumaran, Martin Sachse, Marcio Barrios, Dan, AimelyneM, Matt Sullivan, Delnatte Pierre-Antoine, Jake Smith, Eugen Tudorancea, Iris, David Trinh, simonstl, Ray Daly, Uros Gruber, Justin Myers, Shai Zonis, Mom & Dad, Devin Clark, Dennis Palmer, Brian Panahi Johnson, Josh Marshall, Marshall, Dennis Kerr, Matt Steele, Erik Slagter, Sacah, Justin Rainbow, Christian Nilsson, Delapouite, D.Pereira, Nicolas Hoizey, George V. Reilly, Dan Reeves, Bruno Laturner, Chad Jennings, Shane King, Jeremiah Lee Cohick, od3n, Stan Yamane, Marko Vucinic, Jim B, Stephen Collins, Ægir Þorsteinsson, Eric Pederson, Owain, Nathan Smith, Jeanetteurphy, Alexandre ELISÉ, Chris Peterson, Rik Watson, Luke Matthews, Justin Lowery, Morten Nielsen, Vernon Kesner, Chetan Shenoy, Paul Tregoing, Marc Grabanski, Dion Almaer, Andrew Sullivan, Keith Elsass, Tom Burke, Brian Ashenfelter, David Stuart, Karl Swedberg, Graeme, Brandon Hays, John Christopher, Gior, manoj reddy, Chad Smith, Jared Harbour, Minoru TODA, Chris Wigley, Daniel Mee, Mike, Handyface, Alex Jahraus, Carl Furrow, Rob Foulkrod, Max Shishkin, Leigh Penny Jr., Robert Ferguson, Mike van Hoenselaar, Hasse Schougaard, rajan venkataguru, Jeff Adams, Trae Robbins, Rolf Langenhuijzen, Jorge Antunes, Alex Koloskov, Hugh Greenish, Tim Jones, Jose Ochoa, Michael Brennan-White, Naga Harish Muvva, Barkóczi Dávid, Kitt Hodsden, Paul McGraw, Sascha Goldhofer, Andrew Metcalf, Markus Krogh, Michael Mathews, Matt Jared, Juanfran, Georgie Kirschner, Kenny Lee, Ted Zhang, Amit Pahwa, Inbal Sinai, Dan Raine, Schabse Laks, Michael Tervoort, Alexandre Abreu, Alan Joseph Williams, NicolasD, Cindy Wong, Reg Braithwaite, LocalPCGuy, Jon Friskics, Chris Merriman, John Pena, Jacob Katz, Sue Lockwood, Magnus Johansson, Jeremy Crapsey, Grzegorz Pawłowski, nico nuzzaci, Christine Wilks, Hans Bergren, charles montgomery, Ariel בר-לבב Fogel, Ivan Kolev, Daniel Campos, Hugh Wood, Christian Bradford, Frédéric Harper, Ionuţ Dan Popa, Jeff Trimble, Rupert Wood, Trey Carrico, Pancho Lopez, Joël kuijten, Tom A Marra, Jeff

Jewiss, Jacob Rios, Paolo Di Stefano, Soledad Penades, Chris Gerber, Andrey Dolganov, Wil Moore III, Thomas Martineau, Kareem, Ben Thouret, Udi Nir, Morgan Laupies, jory carson-burson, Nathan L Smith, Eric Damon Walters, Derry Lozano-Hoyland, Geoffrey Wiseman, mkeehner, KatieK, Scott MacFarlane, Brian LaShomb, Adrien Mas, christopher ross, Ian Littman, Dan Atkinson, Elliot Jobe, Nick Dozier, Peter Wooley, John Hoover, dan, Martin A. Jackson, Héctor Fernando Hurtado, andy ennamorato, Paul Seltmann, Melissa Gore, Dave Pollard, Jack Smith, Philip Da Silva, Guy Israeli, @megalithic, Damian Crawford, Felix Gliesche, April Carter Grant, Heidi, jim tierney, Andrea Giammarchi, Nico Vignola, Don Jones, Chris Hartjes, Alex Howes, john gibbon, David J. Groom, BBox, Yu *Dilys* Sun, Nate Steiner, Brandon Satrom, Brian Wyant, Wesley Hales, Ian Pouncey, Timothy Kevin Oxley, George Terezakis, sanjay raj, Jordan Harband, Marko McLion, Wolfgang Kaufmann, Pascal Peuckert, Dave Nugent, Markus Liebelt, Welling Guzman, Nick Cooley, Daniel Mesquita, Robert Syvarth, Chris Coyier, Rémy Bach, Adam Dougal, Alistair Duggin, David Loidolt, Ed Richer, Brian Chenault, GoldFire Studios, Carles Andrés, Carlos Cabo, Yuya Saito, roberto ricardo, Barnett Klane, Mike Moore, Kevin Marx, Justin Love, Joe Taylor, Paul Dijou, Michael Kohler, Rob Cassie, Mike Tierney, Cody Leroy Lindley, tofuji, Shimon Schwartz, Raymond, Luc De Brouwer, David Hayes, Rhys Brett-Bowen, Dmitry, Aziz Khoury, Dean, Scott Tolinski - Level Up, Clement Boirie, Djordje Lukic, Anton Kotenko, Rafael Corral, Philip Hurwitz, Jonathan Pidgeon, Jason Campbell, Joseph C., SwiftOne, Jan Hohner, Derick Bailey, getify, Daniel Cousineau, Chris Charlton, Eric Turner, David Turner, Joël Galeran, Dharma Vagabond, adam, Dirk van Bergen, dave ♥♫★ furf, Vedran Zakanj, Ryan McAllen, Natalie Patrice Tucker, Eric J. Bivona, Adam Spooner, Aaron Cavano, Kelly Packer, Eric J, Martin Drenovac, Emilis, Michael Pelikan, Scott F. Walter, Josh Freeman, Brandon Hudgeons, vijay chennupati, Bill Glennon, Robin R., Troy Forster, otaku_coder, Brad, Scott, Frederick Ostrander, Adam Brill, Seb Flippence, Michael Anderson, Jacob, Adam Randlett, Standard, Joshua Clanton, Sebastian Kouba, Chris Deck, SwordFire, Hannes Papenberg, Richard Woeber, hnzz, Rob Crowther, Jedidiah Broadbent, Sergey Chernyshev, Jay-Ar Jamon, Ben Combee, luciano bonachela, Mark Tomlinson, Kit Cambridge, Michael Melgares, Jacob Adams, Adrian Bruinhout, Bev Wieber, Scott Puleo, Thomas Herzog, April Leone, Daniel Mizieliński, Kees van Ginkel, Jon Abrams, Erwin Heiser, Avi Laviad, David newell, Jean-Francois Turcot, Niko Roberts, Erik Dana, Charles Neill, Aaron Holmes, Grzegorz Ziółkowski, Nathan Youngman, Timothy, Jacob Mather, Michael Allan, Mohit Seth, Ryan Ewing, Benjamin Van Treese, Marcelo Santos, Denis Wolf, Phil Keys, Chris Yung, Timo Tijhof, Martin Lekvall, Agendine, Greg Whitworth, Helen Humphrey, Dougal Campbell, Johannes Harth, Bruno Girin, Brian Hough, Darren Newton, Craig McPheat, Olivier Tille, Dennis Roethig, Mathias Bynens, Brendan Stromberger, sundeep, John Meyer, Ron Male, John F Croston III, gigante, Carl Bergenhem, B.J. May, Rebekah Tyler, Ted Foxberry, Jordan Reese, Terry Suitor, afeliz, Tom Kiefer, Darragh Duffy, Kevin Vanderbeken, Andy Pearson, Simon Mac Donald, Abid Din, Chris Joel, Tomas Theunissen, David Dick, Paul Grock, Brandon Wood, John Weis, dgrebb, Nick Jenkins, Chuck Lane, Johnny Megahan, marzsman, Tatu Tamminen, Geoffrey Knauth, Alexander Tarmolov, Jeremy Tymes, Chad Auld, Sean Parmelee, Rob Staenke, Dan Bender, Yannick derwa, Joshua Jones, Geert Plaisier, Tom LeZotte, Christen Simpson, Stefan Bruvik, Justin Falcone, Carlos Santana, Michael Weiss, Pablo Villoslada, Peter deHaan, Dimitris Iliopoulos, seyDoggy, Adam Jordens, Noah Kantrowitz, Amol M, Matthew Winnard, Dirk Ginader, Phinam Bui, David Rapson, Andrew Baxter, Florian Bougel, Michael George, Alban Escalier, Daniel Sellers, Sasha Rudan, John Green, Robert Kowalski, David I. Teixeira (@ditma, Charles Carpenter, Justin Yost, Sam S, Denis Ciccale, Kevin Sheurs, Yannick Croissant, Pau Fracés, Stephen McGowan, Shawn Searcy, Chris Ruppel, Kevin Lamping, Jessica Campbell, Christopher Schmitt, Sablons, Jonathan Reisdorf, Bunni Gek, Teddy Huff, Michael Mullany, Michael Fürstenberg, Carl Henderson, Rick Yoesting, Scott Nichols, Hernán Ciudad, Andrew Maier, Mike Stapp, Jesse Shawl, Sérgio Lopes, jsulak, Shawn Price, Joel Clermont, Chris Ridmann, Sean Timm, Jason Finch, Aiden Montgomery, Elijah Manor, Derek Gathright, Jesse Harlin, Dillon Curry, Courtney Myers, Diego Cadenas, Arne de Bree, João Paulo Dubas, James Taylor, Philipp Kraeutli, Mihai Păun, Sam Gharegozlou, joshjs, Matt Murchison, Eric Windham, Timo Behrmann, Andrew Hall, joshua price, and Théophile Villard.

This book series is being written in the open source, including editing and production. We owe Github a debt of gratitude for making that sort of thing possible for the community!

Thank you again to all the countless folks I didn't name but who I nonetheless owe thanks. May this book series be "owned" by all of us and serve to contribute to increasing awareness and understanding of the JavaScript language, to the benefit of all current and future community contributors.

About the Author

Kyle Simpson is an Open Web Evangelist from Austin, TX. He's passionate about JavaScript, HTML5, real-time/peer-to-peer communications, and web performance. Otherwise, he's probably bored by it. Kyle is an author, workshop trainer, tech speaker, and avid OSS community member.

Colophon

The cover font for *Scope and Closures* is Interstate. The text font is Adobe Minion Pro; the heading font is Adobe Myriad Condensed; and the code font is Dalton Maag's Ubuntu Mono.

Get even more for your money.

Join the O'Reilly Community, and register the O'Reilly books you own. It's free, and you'll get:

- $4.99 ebook upgrade offer
- 40% upgrade offer on O'Reilly print books
- Membership discounts on books and events
- Free lifetime updates to ebooks and videos
- Multiple ebook formats, DRM FREE
- Participation in the O'Reilly community
- Newsletters
- Account management
- 100% Satisfaction Guarantee

Signing up is easy:

1. **Go to: oreilly.com/go/register**
2. **Create an O'Reilly login.**
3. **Provide your address.**
4. **Register your books.**

Note: English-language books only

To order books online:

oreilly.com/store

For questions about products or an order:

orders@oreilly.com

To sign up to get topic-specific email announcements and/or news about upcoming books, conferences, special offers, and new technologies:

elists@oreilly.com

For technical questions about book content:

booktech@oreilly.com

To submit new book proposals to our editors:

proposals@oreilly.com

O'Reilly books are available in multiple DRM-free ebook formats. For more information:

oreilly.com/ebooks

O'REILLY®

Spreading the knowledge of innovators   oreilly.com

CPSIA information can be obtained at www.ICGtesting.com
Printed in the USA
LVOW01s2057020414

380034LV00019B/102/P